*Speech–Language Path*

*Guide to Home Health Care*

# Speech–Language Pathologist's Guide to Home Health Care

ROBERTA B. PIERCE, MAT, CCCSP

ACADEMIC PRESS

San Diego  London  Boston  New York  Sydney  Tokyo  Toronto

Copyright © 2000 by ACADEMIC PRESS

Academic Press
*a Harcourt Science and Technology Company*
525 B Street, Suite 1900, San Diego, California 92101-4495
http://www.academicpress.com

Academic Press Limited
24-28 Oval Road, London NW1 7DX, UK
http://www.hbuk.co.uk/ap/

Library of Congress Catalog Card Number: 99-68015

International Standard Book Number: 0-12-554830-3

PRINTED IN UNITED STATES OF AMERICA
00  01  02  03  04  05   MM   9  8  7  6  5  4  3  2  1

# CONTENTS

*Chapter 4*
# DOCUMENTATION

*Chapter 5*
# COUNSELING THE PATIENT AND FAMILY

*Chapter 6*
# TREATMENT PROCEDURES

*Chapter 7*
# THERAPY ACTIVITIES: LANGUAGE

*Chapter 8*
# THERAPY ACTIVITIES: ARTICULATION

## Appendix

# *Introduction*

# Introduction

## "THERE'S NO PLACE LIKE HOME"

During the last decade, there has been an increasing interest and involvement in home health care. There is no doubt that patients recover better in the peace and quiet and familiar surroundings of their own homes. In this age of escalating medical costs, caring for the patient in the home is far less expensive than in hospitals or nursing homes.

In reality, home care is not something new that our generation invented. It is the oldest form of health care under the sun. As Janet Nassif states in *The Home HealthCare Solution: A Complete Consumer Guide* (1985), "Before the advent of our modern health care system, most people began life at home and ended it there too. When they were downed by illness, injury, old age, and infirmity, they were cared for in their own homes by family, friends, and the family physician" (p. 3).

The role of the home health care team is twofold: to treat the patient and to provide training for the caregivers to help them cope with the challenges of caring for their loved ones in the home.

# THE HOME HEALTH CARE TEAM

Referral for home health services usually begins with the Social Worker, Case Manager, or Discharge Planner affiliated with an acute care hospital. The referral is made when the patient is discharged from the hospital. The home health agency needs "doctor's orders" to get reimbursement for any services provided. An intake worker, usually the RN assigned to the case, makes the initial visit to the home to assess patient and family needs. Any or all of the following services may be provided:

1.  **Skilled nursing**. An RN will be required to perform skilled nursing services, such as changing dressing on wounds, administering drugs, and monitoring the patient's health. The RN teaches the family to perform basic health care services, such as taking temperature and pulse rate, and is available to answer the many questions the patient and family ask. The RN Case Manager usually handles all paperwork and communication directly with the physician's office.

2.  **Home health aides**. The home health aide is trained to assist the patient with personal care needs such as bathing, toileting, grooming, dressing, eating, and mobility. The aide can be taught to follow through on exercise protocols developed by the rehabilitation specialists.

3.  **Rehabilitation specialists**: The Physical Therapist, Occupational Therapist, and Speech–Language Pathologist. In their respective roles, they work to restore, maintain, and enhance the patient's abilities and to train family members to assist in the patient's rehabilitation.

# ADVANTAGES OF HOME HEALTH SPEECH–LANGUAGE PATHOLOGY

There is a strong push in the current literature to make our treatment more relevant, to focus on functionality. The home health therapist has the advantage of seeing the patient in a REAL-LIFE situation. It is easier to work on functional everyday needs in the patient's home than in a somewhat artificial clinical setting.

The patient and the caregivers are frequently more appreciative of the therapy rendered because the therapist has come to the patient's home. They are often more willing to follow through on suggestions and recommendations. This may be because the recommendations are more meaningful and appropriate.

For the home health therapist, it is easier to get a more accurate perspective of the patient's communication abilities and needs, mobility, and self-help needs in the home setting than it is in the hospital or clinic.

# DISADVANTAGES OF HOME HEALTH
# SPEECH–LANGUAGE PATHOLOGY

Home health patients are generally more impaired than patients seen in outpatient rehabilitation facilities. Most home health agencies and third-party payers have very specific and strict guidelines requiring that patients be homebound to be eligible for services. This generally means they are bedridden or at least confined to a wheelchair. They are restricted from leaving the home for church, social functions, or routine chores such as going to the grocery store or beauty parlor. In most instances, a doctor's appointment is the only outing allowed.

With changes in reimbursement systems, patients are being discharged from acute-care hospitals sooner, in some cases prematurely. Not only are home health patients more severely involved, but they are more likely to be not medically stable when home health services begin.

To compound these problems, the frequency and duration of visits allowed by health insurance or Medicare reimbursement policies are often restricted. The reality of home health is that, in most cases, the patient can be seen only two or three times per week for 2 to 9 weeks. The goals of therapy must be different, and the family must be taught to perform many of the tasks that were traditionally done by the therapist.

Another disadvantage of home health therapy is that you are on the patient's "turf"; therefore, there may be more distractions (e.g., dog barking, TV blaring, dishwasher running) than you would have if the patient came to your office or outpatient clinic.

Similarly, it is not as convenient logistically to do therapy in a patient's home. More planning for the treatment sessions and preparation of therapy materials must be done beforehand, where the therapist has a wider variety of materials and a copying machine "back at the office." Most home settings compromise the "traditional" seating arrangements of working with the patient across a therapy table. Often therapy must be provided to patients who are in bed or on the couch. Physical therapy is at the greatest disadvantage in the home as compared to a well-equipped PT gym with modern equipment, parallel bars, and exercise mats. Occupational therapy, on the other hand, is considerably better able to assess and teach activities of daily living and modifications/adaptations in the home.

# *Types of Impairments*

# *Types of Impairments*

## APHASIA

Aphasia is the term used to describe loss or impairment of language functions resulting from damage to the brain. Neurological damage may result from any of the following conditions:

1. **CVA** — thrombosis, hemorrhage, or embolism.
2. **Trauma** — closed head injury or open wound.
3. **Infectious disease** — meningitis, encephalitis.
4. **Poisons or intoxication** — drugs or alcohol, purposefully or accidentally.
5. **Brain tumor**.

There are a number of good textbooks on diagnosis and treatment of aphasia. The home health clinician should be familiar with the following:

*Aphasia: A Clinical Approach*, by John Rosenbek, Leonard LaPointe, and Robert Wertz (Pro-Ed, Austin, TX: 1989).

*The Assessment of Aphasia and Related Disorders*, 2nd ed., by Harold Goodglass and Edith Kaplan (Lea and Febiger, Philadelphia, 1983).

*Acquired Aphasia*, 2nd ed., by Martha Sarno (Academic Press, New York, 1991).

*Approaches to the Treatment of Aphasia*, by Nancy Helms-Estabrooks and Audrey Holland (Singular Publishing Group, San Diego, 1998).

Aphasia will affect to some degree the individual's competence in each of the four communication modalities:

1. **Auditory** — understanding spoken language.
2. **Lexical** — understanding written language.
3. **Oral** — formulating spoken language.
4. **Graphic** — formulating written language.

In the chapter on treatment procedures (see Chapter 6), remediation of language impairments will be discussed under the modalities of auditory comprehension, reading comprehension, and expressive language.

The patient with aphasia is likely to exhibit some or all of the following characteristics:

1. **Anomia** — difficulty retrieving the names for things.

2. **Circumlocution** — talking around a subject in an attempt to self-cue retrieval of a certain word.

3. **Perseveration** — saying a word or phrase repeatedly inappropriately.

4. **Paraphasias**.

   *Literal* — disorganization of sounds or syllables within words ("batel" for "table").

   *Semantic/verbal* – in-class substitution of one word for another of similar meaning ("I eat soup with a fork").

   *Neologistic* — using jargon, nonsense words ("He filcomed my blitzcat").

   *Syntactic* — transposition of words or phrases ("Why do you have that face on your smile?").

5. **Comprehension Problems**.

   *Auditory agnosia* — hear it but don't understand what they hear.

   *Visual agnosia* — see it but don't recognize what they see.

   *Tactile agnosia* — feel it but can't identify by touch alone.

6. **Apraxia and/or Dysarthria**.

Historically, there have been a number of different approaches to classification of aphasias. In the earliest writings (e.g., Weisenburg and McBride, 1935), patients were classified as predominantly receptive, predominantly expressive, expressive-receptive, or global. Patients with "predominantly receptive aphasia" experience more difficulty understanding spoken and written communication than they do in speaking or writing. Conversely, patients with "predominantly expressive aphasia" experience more difficulty formulating spoken and written communication than they do in understanding spoken speech or written language. "Expressive-receptive" patients have about equal involvement in input and output. Patients with "global aphasia" respond minimally because they have severe problems with both input and output.

Current popular classification systems categorize aphasics as "non-fluent" or "fluent." Patients with non-fluent aphasia have word retrieval difficulties. Their speech is halting, filled with pauses, as they search for the right words to express themselves. They usually respond in single words or short phrases. Words may be mispronounced or painstakingly articulated. Patients with fluent aphasia characteristically talk a lot but say little because their speech is full of paraphasias. They do not monitor their speech output, so they tend to think that they are communicating effectively and that their listeners are to blame for not understanding them or responding appropriately. Fluent aphasics usually have normal prosody and normal phrase length.

Other classification systems are derived from the patient's responses to various testing protocols. The differentiating characteristics of the major "syndromes," according to Goodglass and Kaplan (1983b), are charted in Figure 1. The research of Drs. Hannah and Antonio Damasio, essential to differential diagnosis, is depicted in Figure 1.

| Classification | Language deficits | Fluent/ nonfluent | Auditory comprehension | Naming | Repetition | Localization of lesion |
|---|---|---|---|---|---|---|
| Global Aphasia | Severe impairment of all language abilities | Nonfluent | Extremely limited | Severely impaired | Severely impaired | Varies, usually extensive |
| Broca's Aphasia | Telegraphic utterances; abnormal prosody; frequent coexistence with apraxia | Nonfluent | Less impaired than oral expression | Mildly to severely impaired | Mildly to severely impaired | Left lower posterior frontal lobe (Brodman's area 44); may involve lower portion of motor strip and territory anterior and superior to area 44 |
| Transcortical Motor Aphasia | Severe impairment of spontaneous speech | Nonfluent | Mildly to moderately impaired | Better than spontaneous speech | Better than spontaneous speech | May be superior to, or deep within, Broca's area (Brodman's area 44) |
| Wernicke's Aphasia | Good articulation; longer phrase length; grammatical but incorrect; paraphasias, neologisms, and jargon | Fluent | Severely impaired | Mildly to severely impaired | Mildly to severely impaired | Posterior region of the left superior temporal gyrus, but may extend into the second temporal gyrus and adjacent parietal region, especially the angular gyrus |
| Transcortical Sensory Aphasia | Good articulation and phrase length; lots of paraphasias and severely lacking in nouns | Fluent | Mildly to moderately impaired | Moderately to severely impaired | Within normal limits | Extensive lesion in posterior portion of the middle temporal gyrus that extends into visual and auditory association cortex and perhaps into the angular gyrus |
| Conduction Aphasia | Good articulation, phrase length, syntax, and prosody | Fluent | Mildly to moderately impaired | Mildly to severely impaired | Severely impaired | Supramarginal gyrus, Brodman's area 40 and the superior temporal lobe |
| Anomic Aphasia | Good articulation, phrase length, syntax, and prosody | Fluent | Mildly to moderately impaired | Mildly to severely impaired | Mildly to moderately impaired | Focal lesion, usually in the angular gyrus or the second temporal gyrus |

**Figure 1 –
Classification of
Aphasias.**

Based on Goodglass and Kaplan (1983b), A. Damasio (1991), and H. Damasio (1991).

In addition to the seven major classifications of aphasia detailed in Figure 1, the clinician needs to be aware of the following:

1. **Mixed Non-Fluent Aphasia.** Symptoms are between Global and Broca's.

2. **Alexia with Agraphia.** Impaired reading and writing with no auditory comprehension or oral expressive deficits.

3. **Atypical or "Pure" Aphasias.** Impaired performance in a single input or output modality with essentially intact performance in all other modalities.

   a. Aphemia (Broca, 1861) — Apraxia of speech

   b. Alexia without Agraphia — "pure alexia"

   c. Pure Word Deafness

   d. Pure Agraphia

4. **Subcortical Aphasias**. Similar to other aphasias but with persisting right hemiplegia and dysarthria.

5. **Crossed Aphasia**. Right hemiplegia and aphasia in a left-handed person who suffered a left hemisphere lesion or left hemiplegia and aphasia in a right-handed person who suffered a right hemisphere lesion.

Rosenbek *et al.* (1989) describe seven communication disorders that are somewhat similar to aphasia but that must be differentiated from aphasia.

1. The Language of Confusion
2. Dementia
3. Right-Hemisphere Impairment
4. Schizophrenia
5. Environmental Influence on Language
6. Apraxia of Speech
7. Dysarthria

The home health speech–language pathologist will frequently work with patients who have aphasia, apraxia, and/or dysarthria. Occasionally, a patient with one of the above disorders will be referred for services. Differential diagnosis, including medical and neurological information, is extremely important. Medicare guidelines for home health speech–language pathology services require that there be a good prognosis for improvement. It is difficult to justify home health treatment for the patient with Language of Confusion, Dementia, Schizophrenia, or Environmental Influence on Language. Treatment should include diagnostic testing, patient/family counseling, and patient/family education. In summary, Rosenbek *et al.*, (1989) define aphasia accordingly:

> Aphasia is an impairment, due to acquired and recent damage of the central nervous system, of the ability to comprehend and formulate language. It is a multimodality disorder represented by a variety of impairments in auditory comprehension, reading, oral-expressive language, and writing. The disrupted language may be influenced by physiological inefficiency or impaired cognition, but it cannot be explained by dementia, sensory loss, or motor dysfunction. (p. 53)

# APRAXIA

Throughout the literature, there are excellent descriptions of the motor speech disorder *apraxia*. Patients with **oral apraxia** will have difficulty imitating tongue and lip movements. Patients with **verbal apraxia**, more commonly called **apraxia of speech**, will have difficulty sequencing the movements of the articulators for production of speech. The home health speech pathologist should be familiar with these textbooks:

*Motor Speech Disorders*, by Frederick Darley, Arnold Aronson, and Joe Brown (W. B. Saunders, Philadelphia, 1975).

*Apraxia of Speech in Adults: The Disorder and Its Management*, by Robert Wertz, Leonard LaPointe, and John Rosenbek (Singular Publishing Group, San Diego, 1991).

*Disorders of Motor Speech: Assessment, Treatment, and Clinical Characterization*, by Donald Robin, Kathryn Yorkston, and David Beukelman (Paul H. Brookes, Baltimore, 1996).

All of these authors describe apraxia of speech as a motor planning and sequencing disorder wherein the patient knows what he wants to say but is unable to program the articulators in the correct sequence to utter the desired response. Apraxia of speech may be mild, moderate, or severe.

Wertz *et al.* (1991) define apraxia of speech by four vital clinical characteristics:

1. Speech is effortful, with trial-and-error groping, articulatory movements, and attempts at self-correction.

2. There is dysprosody unrelieved by extended periods of normal rhythm, stress, and intonation.

3. There is articulatory inconsistency on repeated productions of the same utterance.

4. There is obvious difficulty initiating utterances.

Huskins (1986/1988) states that it is difficult to accurately diagnose apraxia of speech in very severe cases because the patient must be able to produce some speech for the clinician to analyze. The criteria for diagnosis in very severe cases are: "absence of speech in the presence of moderate to good language performance on aphasia tests, and the absence of any neuromuscular impairment of an anarthric (dysarthric) nature" (Huskins, 1986/1988, p. 11). The patient can spontaneously chew, swallow, cough, and smile normally, but may be unable to phonate voluntarily. He cannot imitate speech, read aloud, or name pictures. Some patients with severe apraxia of speech may have made a choice to be mute, realizing that attempts to communicate will likely fail. Some may produce automatic speech, including swearing fluently and clearly, although functional speech is virtually absent. Other severely apraxic patients are further handicapped by a recurrent utterance or perseveration on a word or nonsense syllable.

Darley *et al.* (1975) describe the clinical features of apraxia of speech as follows:

1. The apraxic patient effortfully gropes to find the correct articulatory postures and sequences of them. He often behaves as though uncertain of where his tongue is or of how to move it in a given direction or to a given position. . . .

2. Such articulatory difficulty involves consonant phonemes more often than vowel phonemes.

3. The articulation errors are inconsistent and highly variable, not referable to specific muscle dysfunction.

4. The articulatory errors are primarily substitutions, additions, repetitions, and prolongations — essentially complications of the act of articulation. Errors of simplification, such as distortions and omissions, are relatively much less frequent.

5. Analysis of substitution errors by distinctive features (place, manner, voicing, and oral–nasal characteristics) indicates that the majority of errors are close approximations of the target sounds. . . .

6. Articulatory errors appear to be at times perseverative, with recurrence of phonemes recently articulated, and at times anticipatory, with the premature introduction of a phoneme that appears in a subsequent word. . . .

7. In attempting to produce a difficult cluster of consonants, the patient may simplify his task by inserting a schwa between the elements, as in pronouncing "stuh-rike" for "strike."

8. Patients with apraxia of speech can recognize their articulatory errors beyond random guess. (p. 262–264)

# DYSARTHRIA

In *Motor Speech Disorders*, Darley *et al.* (1975) state the following:

The efficient execution of oral communication requires the smooth sequencing and coordination of three basic processes:

1. The organization of concepts and their symbolic formulation and expression.

2. The externalization of thought in speech through the concurrent motor functions of respiration, phonation, resonance, articulation, and prosody.

3. The programming of these motor skills in the volitional production of individual speech sounds and their combination into sequences to form words. (p. 1)

Neurological damage and/or deterioration may affect any one of these three processes or all three to varying degrees. When the impairment is basically to language function (#1), the result is **aphasia**. When the impairment affects speech production because of weakness or paralysis in the muscles used for breathing, producing and modifying sound, articulating sounds, and affecting rhythm, rate, and intonation patterns (#2), the result is **dysarthria**. When the impairment affects the patient's ability to produce and sequence articulatory movements (#3), the result is **apraxia of speech**.

Dysarthria refers to a group of motor speech disorders involving disturbances in muscular control. There is damage to the central or peripheral nervous system, resulting in some degree of weakness, slowness, incoordination, or altered muscle tone.

Darley *et al.* (1975) review the literature regarding the classification of dysarthrias and present six designations based on neuromuscular manifestations (see Figure 2).

Examination for motor dysfunction involves assessment of muscle strength, speed of movement, range of excursion, accuracy of movement, motor steadiness (tremor or random involuntary movement), and muscle tone. Dysarthria may affect — to varying degrees in different individuals — respiration, phonation, resonation, articulation, and/or prosody. Because dysarthric speech results from impairment to the underlying neuromus-

| Designation | Explanation |
|---|---|
| Flaccid dysarthria | Lower motor neuron lesion |
| Spastic dysarthria | Bilateral upper motor neuron lesion |
| Ataxic dysarthria | Cerebellar or cerebellar pathway lesion |
| Hypokinetic dysarthria<br>in parkinsonism | Extrapyramidal lesion |
| Hyperkinetic dysarthria<br>in chorea<br>in dystonia<br>other | Extrapyramidal lesion<br>quick hyperkinesia<br>slow hyperkinesia |
| Mixed dysarthrias<br>spastic-flaccid in amyotrophic lateral sclerosis<br>spastic–ataxic–hypokinetic in Wilson's disease<br>variable in multiple sclerosis<br>others | Lesions of multiple systems |

**Figure 2 – Classification of Dysarthrias.**

Reprinted with permission from Darley *et al.* (1975).

cular system, the patient is very likely to have some degree of dysphagia. The assessment protocol should include questions about possible swallowing problems.

It is important for the speech–language pathologist to have sufficient medical and neurological information on the etiology of each individual patient's dysarthria. Goals, specific therapy procedures, and recommendations will be based on whether the patient's condition should respond to therapy or whether it is expected to deteriorate further. For the patient with a good prognosis for recovery, therapy will be geared toward exercises to rehabilitate the weakened muscles. For patients with degenerative medical conditions, therapy will attempt to maintain functional communication for as long as possible and prepare the patient and family for augmentative communication when verbalization is no longer possible.

Dysarthria may result from CVA, head injury, ALS, Huntington's Chorea, Polio, Cerebellar Ataxia, Cerebral Palsy, Myasthenia Gravis, Parkinson's Disease, Bell's Palsy, Friedreich's Ataxia, Wilson's Disease, Tourette's Syndrome, Multiple Sclerosis, Guillain–Barré Syndrome, Pseudobulbar Palsy, and Encephalitis. Dysarthria may also result from damage to nerves or muscle groups caused by cancer, head or neck surgery, brain tumor, drug overdose, or environmental toxins.

Clinically, the most common characteristic of dysarthria is slurred speech. Articulation of consonants and vowels is distorted and indistinct. The errors are consistent because they result from weakness or paralysis of the musculature. The voice may be hypernasal, pitched too high or too low, monotone, or weak. Breath support and breath control may make it difficult to project the voice. Rate may be too slow or too fast.

Goals for treatment and specific therapy techniques will depend upon the etiology of the dysarthria, the patient's speech and voice dysfunctions, and the prognosis for improvement or recovery.

# RIGHT-HEMISPHERE IMPAIRMENT

Neurological damage to the right hemisphere of the brain, resulting from stroke, head injury, or tumor, will affect the left side of the body. The person usually has behavioral, intellectual, and emotional changes, which are referred to as "Cognitive Deficits." Patients and family members need to understand that these cognitive, behavioral, and communication problems occur and they need to be helped to work through them.

Dikengil (1994) states that "injury to the right hemisphere of the brain typically results in cognitive problems, which affect how a person thinks and processes information" (p. 49).

The most common cognitive/communication problems for these individuals are as follows:

1. **Short-term memory**. Long-term memory is usually not affected, but immediate recall of events, discussions, and information may be severely affected.

2. **Attention**. The person may have difficulty concentrating on the task at hand and may be easily distracted by other people, activities, or conversations in the environment.

3. **Pragmatic skills**. The individual may talk too much or too little, not following generally accepted "rules" of conversation.

4. **Expressing thoughts**. The ability to organize thoughts may be disrupted, making it difficult for the individual to express opinions coherently.

5. **Processing information**. There may be delays in the person's ability to process information, leading to delays in responding. Because of the possibility of distractions, it is important to get the person's attention when speaking to them.

6. **Executive functioning**. There may be difficulties in planning, organizing, initiating, and carrying out the steps needed to perform a task. The person's ability to sequence the steps, to self-monitor, and to self-correct may be affected.

7. **Judgment**. The person may act impulsively and may have difficulty solving everyday problems because of incomplete or "scrambled" information.

8. **Literal vs. abstract**. The person's ability to think and process abstract information may be impaired, so that he or she may be confused or frustrated by ambiguous or subtle remarks.

9. **Expressing and interpreting emotions**. The individual may laugh or cry inappropriately and may not react as would be expected to happy or sad news. Overreacting or "under"-reacting may occur. Misinterpreting the emotional messages of others, both verbal and nonverbal, may create communication problems.

10. **Inappropriate behavior**. So much of the brain functions to inhibit inappropriate responses. When there has been damage to the right hemisphere, the person may laugh, cry, curse, or display anger or affection inappropriately.

Essential information on Right-Hemisphere Impairments can be found in:
*Right Hemisphere Communication Disorders: Theory and Management*, by Connie Tompkins (Singular Publishing Group, San Diego, 1995).
"Right Hemisphere Syndrome," by Penelope S. Myers and E. Louise Mackisack in *Aphasia and Related Neurogenic Language Disorders* (Leonard LaPointe, ed.; Thieme Medical Publishers, New York, 1990).
*Right Brain Stroke: A Guide for the Patient and Family*, by Marla Knight (Interactive Therapeutics, Stow, OH, 1996).

# TRAUMATIC BRAIN INJURY

In recent years, there has been a significant increase in the number of patients with head injury in all rehabilitation settings. This increase appears to be directly related to advances in medical technology and in emergency (trauma) medical procedures. Evidence suggests that more individuals are "surviving" traumatic accidents because the rescue teams are trained to begin effective life-saving techniques at the scene, helicopters can transport the patients more quickly to emergency rooms or trauma centers, and awaiting physicians can more quickly and accurately diagnose and treat the severely injured.

The leading causes of traumatic brain injury are: (1) vehicular accidents, including automobiles, motorcycles, and bicycles, and (2) gunshot wounds or blunt instrument trauma, such as getting hit in the head with a baseball bat or tire iron. Occasionally, the therapist may also encounter patients whose head injury was caused by a fall from a high place, a dive into shallow water, or a natural disaster, such as an earthquake or tornado.

Damage from head injury is usually more diffuse than that from stroke or brain tumor. The patient is almost always comatose for a period of time varying from a few minutes to weeks or months. There may be a wide variety of residual impairments, depending upon the type, severity, and extent of damage to the brain.

Cynthia Jones and Janis Lorman (1988) have written an excellent booklet, *Traumatic Brain Injury: A Guide for the Patient and Family*, which describes in easy-to-understand terms how the brain works as a control center and what happens in various types of head injuries. They state:

> With localized brain injuries, specific problems may be noted. These may include paralysis, language or speech problems, and changes in the senses, such as decreased vision, hearing, smell, taste, and/or feeling. With more generalized brain injury, the problems cover a broader range. Problems may include decreased awareness and alertness, memory loss, decreased orientation, difficulty with reasoning, lack of insight, behavioral changes, poor problem-solving and judgment — as well as difficulty with thinking skills (or cognition) in general. When the brain stem or cerebellum is injured, other problem areas are noted. There may be difficulty breathing, swallowing, and coordinating muscle movements. (p. 10)

Except in isolated injuries such as a gunshot wound to the head, there are often broken bones, internal injuries, and open wounds, which require and receive immediate medical attention. The existence and extent of head injury may not be recognized until after initial emergency medical treatment has been completed.

The patient with traumatic brain injury is very likely to have some degree of impairment in each of the following areas:

1. **Weakness or paralysis in the right, left, or both sides of the body**. If the patient is comatose for a long period of time, he will usually lose much of the muscle tissue and tone in the extremities. If the injury occurs at the level of the brain stem, balance will be a significant problem, making it difficult to stand or walk.

2. **Speech and language deficits**. The patient may have aphasia, apraxia, and/or dysarthria.

3. **Cognitive deficits**. The recovering head injury patient may have difficulty in one or more of the skills necessary for learning new information and recalling previously learned information. These skills include but are not limited to:

   a. alertness and attention span

   b. orientation to person, place, and time

   c. perception and discrimination involving all the senses

   d. short-term and long-term memory

   e. emotional/social/behavioral control

   f. judgment, insight, problem solving, and reasoning

The Levels of Cognitive Functioning Scale (Hagen *et al.*, 1979) was developed by the head injury treatment team at the Rancho Los Amigos Hospital in Los Angeles, California. The stages in the recovery process are predictable; however, it is not possible to predict how quickly an individual patient will move through the stages or what the eventual recovery will be.

   I.    NO RESPONSE: Unresponsive to any stimulus.

   II.   GENERALIZED RESPONSE: Limited, inconsistent, non-purposeful responses, often to pain only.

   III.  LOCALIZED RESPONSE: Purposeful responses; may follow simple commands, may focus on presented object.

   IV.   CONFUSED, AGITATED: Heightened state of activity; confusion, disorientation, aggressive behavior; unable to do self-care; unaware of present events; agitation appears related to internal confusion.

   V.    CONFUSED, INAPPROPRIATE, NON-AGITATED: Appears alert; responds to commands; distractible, does not concentrate on task; agitated responses to external stimuli; verbally inappropriate; does not learn new information.

   VI.   CONFUSED APPROPRIATE: Good directed behavior, needs cueing; can relearn old skills such as Activities of Daily Living (ADLs); serious memory problems; some awareness of self and others.

   VII.  AUTOMATIC APPROPRIATE: Robot-like appropriate behavior, minimal confusion; shallow recall; poor insight into condition; initiates tasks but needs structure; poor judgment, problem-solving and planning skills.

VIII. PURPOSEFUL APPROPRIATE: Alert, oriented; recalls and integrates past events; learns new activities and can continue without supervision; independent in home and living skills; capable of driving; defects in stress tolerance, judgment, abstract reasoning persist; many function at reduced levels in society.

# DYSPHAGIA

Dysphagia refers to difficulty in swallowing resulting from pathological or neurological disorders.

In pathological dysphagia, normal swallowing is hindered by an obstruction at some point along the swallowing pathway. The patient complains of pain during swallowing and can often identify where the food "gets stuck." Tumors, swelling, scar tissue from surgical procedures, and hiatal hernias are examples of pathological dysphagic conditions. These disorders are diagnosed by X-ray and treated medically or surgically by the physician. The speech pathologist/swallowing therapist could make recommendations regarding food consistencies and positioning the patient to facilitate swallowing.

In neurological dysphagia, normal swallowing is hindered by weakness, paralysis, slowness, or incoordination of the muscles in the swallowing mechanism. Disease or damage affecting the central nervous system or the peripheral nerves can cause neurogenic dysphagia. Most likely to be encountered in the home health setting would be patients with:

1. the progressive degenerative diseases such as Muscular Dystrophy, Amyotrophic Lateral Sclerosis ("Lou Gehrig's Disease"), Myasthenia Gravis, and Parkinson's Disease

2. acute onset from CVA, head injury, or trauma

3. nerve damage from head and neck surgery or radiation

The speech pathologist/swallowing therapist will frequently function as a member of a rehabilitation team. Other team members might include the radiologist, dietician, Occupational Therapist, MD, and RN.

In treating patients for dysphagia, we are truly dealing with possible life-threatening situations. The home health clinician is cautioned to proceed with extreme care and to seek specialized training before attempting to diagnose and treat dysphagic conditions.

The home health speech pathologist should be familiar with the following textbooks:

*Evaluation and Treatment of Swallowing Disorders*, by Jerilyn Logemann (Pro-Ed, Austin, TX, 1983).

*Dysphagia: Diagnosis and Management*, by Michael Groher (Butterworth-Heinemann, Stoneham, MA, 1992).

*The Source for Dysphagia*, by Nancy B. Swigert (LinguiSystems, East Moline, IL, 1996).

# LARYNGECTOMY

Occasionally, the speech–language pathologist will receive a referral for home health therapy for a laryngectomee. The majority of laryngectomees are seen on an outpatient basis in rehabilitation centers, hospital clinics, or private practice. Unless there are extenuating circumstances, laryngectomy patients would not meet the criterion of being "homebound."

The three methods of communication that can be utilized by the laryngectomy patient are esophageal speech, electrolarynx, and tracheoesophageal puncture (TEP).

The speech–language pathologist should have a working knowledge of all three options. Whether or not to have a TEP is a medical management decision that has usually been made by the patient and physician well before the home health speech–language pathologist is consulted. The hospital speech–language pathologist has probably taught the patient and family what they need to know about stoma care, inserting and removing the prosthesis, and troubleshooting. The home health speech–language pathologist would rarely have a role with TEP patients.

In teaching esophageal speech, no matter what the setting, it is extremely helpful to utilize other laryngectomees from the community to meet with new patients and their family members. There is great value to the patient's morale and motivation to actually see and hear someone who has had the same surgery and is able to communicate effectively.

The speech–language pathologist should be familiar with the following books:

*Self-Help for the Laryngectomee*, by Edmund Lauder (Lauder, San Antonio, 1991).

*Clinical Manual of Laryngectomy and Head and Neck Cancer Rehabilitation*, by J. Casper and R. Colton (Singular Publishing Group, San Diego, 1992).

Several pamphlets and booklets are also available through the local chapter of the American Cancer Society or by writing to:

American Cancer Society
1599 Clifton Road N.E.
Atlanta, GA 30329

# DEGENERATIVE NEUROMUSCULAR DISEASES

The speech–language pathologist can play a limited role with patients afflicted with neuromuscular diseases such as Parkinson's, ALS, and multiple sclerosis.

Treatment is not geared toward rehabilitating or making the patient better but, rather, toward maintaining functional communication and eating/drinking for as long as possible. Medicare in particular does not pay for "maintenance therapy" but rarely denies a few home visits predominantly to teach the patient and family facilitation techniques.

Appropriate goals for patients with degenerative neuromuscular diseases would include:

1. To establish an oral muscle exercise program to improve intelligibility of speech and minimize drooling.

2. To counsel patient and family regarding food textures and techniques that enable safe swallowing of foods and liquids.

3. To prepare an augmentative communication system for the patient who is no longer able to verbalize wants and needs.

4. To teach the patient and family techniques to monitor rate of speaking to improve intelligibility.

# *Diagnostics*

# Diagnostics

## PURPOSES

The purposes of the diagnostic session are as follows:
1. To determine the patient's present level of functioning.
2. To identify abilities and disabilities.
3. To define communication deficits for later comparison to document improvement.
4. To establish a plan of treatment, including goals, most appropriate therapy methods and techniques, patient and family counseling needs, and prognosis for improvement.

A number of tests, both formal and informal, are available to the clinician for use during the diagnostic session. The test battery should include assessment of all aspects of verbal and nonverbal communication, as well as sampling writing, spelling, and reading. It would take several hours to measure thoroughly all the necessary communicative skills. This is not practical in the home health setting because patients are not able to tolerate a lengthy test procedure. The speech–language pathologist can adapt key items from a number of existing test batteries to fulfill the purposes of the diagnostic evaluation quickly and effectively.

*Determining the Patient's Present Level of Functioning*

Within the first few minutes, the speech–language pathologist should form a preliminary appraisal of the patient's receptive and expressive communication abilities. Whenever possible, it is helpful to ask the caregivers certain questions in private before even being introduced to the patient. The information obtained will assist the examiner in selecting the type of testing that would be most appropriate. These questions also yield useful insight into the family's perception of the patient's communication abilities.

1. **How does he usually let you know what he needs?** This will enable the examiner to know immediately whether the patient is essentially verbal or nonverbal. It will also give significant information regarding how willing the caregiver may or may not be to try to understand the patient's communicative attempts.

2. **Do you feel that she understands what you are trying to say to her?** This will enable the examiner to assess how realistic the family is regarding the patient's actual level of functioning. It is very likely that patients do understand more than they can demonstrate about what is going on around them; and it is also likely that the caregiver, by virtue of having lived with the patient for many years, can assess this aspect more accurately than the therapist, who is unfamiliar with the patient. If family members could only be objective, the question of how much the patient really understands would yield reliable and valuable information. Unfortunately, the responses frequently are at one extreme — i.e., "I'm sure Mother understands everything we say to her; she just can't talk back" (when the patient is obviously in a deep coma) — to the other — "There's no point in even asking him anything; he doesn't know what's going on since his stroke" (when the patient is fairly high-level and just speech- or language-impaired). The perceptive clinician will discover soon enough how much the patient does comprehend and, more importantly, has gained a world of insight into family dynamics by asking this question.

3. **Is his speech the same from day to day or does it seem to be better or worse at times?** It will be important for the speech–language pathologist to know whether there are significant fluctuations in the patient's communicative abilities and whether the patient's responses during the diagnostic procedures are typical. This information will assist the clinician: (1) in masking out the effects of medication and fatigue, and (2) in making recommendations for amount and timing of therapy and daily practice. Specifically, patients are frequently on several medications, and their ability to perform may vary widely with the length of time since the last dosage. Some patients function better early in the morning before they have a chance to become fatigued, whereas others are less responsive early in the morning. Some patients will respond better to short practice sessions (5–10 minutes) throughout the day; others will respond optimally to one or two longer practice sessions (30 minutes) per day.

In some home situations with limited space (e.g., one-room apartment, mobile home), it is not possible to "interview" the family members "in private." These same questions can be asked delicately in the patient's presence. The information provided by caregivers is important in assessing the patient's present level of functioning.

The patient's response to conversational speech alerts the examiner to which testing protocols will be most appropriate to use. It is always optimal to have scheduled the diagnostic appointment at a time when the family feels that the patient is most likely to be awake and alert. The speech–language pathologist should introduce him/herself slowly and clearly to the patient. Often patients who are moderately aphasic or apraxic can handle "social speech" adequately, so it is important to probe speech and language functions even if the patient appears to converse appropriately. If the patient is nonverbal, the clinician must rely more heavily on body language, facial expressions, gestures, touch, and eye contact to assess how much the patient understands and communicates.

If the patient is verbal, ask him what aspects of communication are most difficult. Patients are usually quite aware of their deficit areas and will give this information readily if they sense that the speech–language pathologist is genuinely concerned with their welfare.

The patient and caregiver generally have a great deal of anxiety about the communicative deficits. The examiner should do everything possible to put them at ease. This can be accomplished by verbalizing what they are experiencing by compassionate statements, such as "You're really having a hard time talking right now," and reassuring statements, such as "I'm here to find out what I can do to help you communicate better."

It is essential to put the patient at ease as much as possible by stating matter-of-factly, "Some of the things I'll ask you to do will be easy for you; some of them will be hard. Just do the best you can on all of them, so I'll know the best way to help you" (Porch, 1967).

## Identifying Abilities and Disabilities

The speech–language pathologist needs to gather as much information as possible as quickly and as gently as possible. A standardized diagnostic battery or a sampling of items from various tests can be used to identify the patient's abilities and disabilities.

The examiner needs to have diagnostic materials at all levels of difficulty readily accessible. Be prepared to assess lower-level skills, such as matching identical objects, gesturing the use of objects, and "yes–no" head-shake or eye-blink responses if the patient is functioning on a low level. Likewise, the examiner must also be prepared to assess high-level language and cognitive skills if the patient is functioning at a higher level. Reading comprehension, motor speech, or other areas that appear to require additional probing can best be addressed at follow-up sessions.

Throughout the diagnostic session, it is important for the speech–language pathologist, the patient, and the caregiver to direct as much attention to the tasks the patient can do well as to the tasks the patient cannot do. For the clinician, the patient's strengths will be the key to selecting the most appropriate therapy techniques for rehabilitating deficits. For the patient and family members, they have been so focused on what the patient cannot do that they are often genuinely surprised at the skills that are still intact. Frequently they were not previously aware that the patient was able to perform certain tasks sampled during the diagnostic procedures.

## Defining Communication Deficits for Later Comparison to Document Improvement

Accountability is increasingly important throughout the health care professions (Frattali, 1998). Accountability measures whether or not, and to what extent, treatment services benefit the patient. It is necessary in the initial diagnostic session to define as accurately as possible exactly what the patient's deficits are so that post-intervention performance can be compared to pre-intervention performance. The ASHA–FACS (Frattali *et al.*, 1995) was developed to provide objective substantive data to third-party payers to document that the patient is making significant gains as a result of the treatment being provided. Demonstrating progress is also crucial in establishing and maintaining a high level of motivation in the patient, the family, and the therapist.

**Establishing a Plan of Treatment**

An essential aim of the diagnostic session is to establish a plan of treatment that sets forth the goals to be accomplished during subsequent therapy. Specific goals will be different for each patient, depending upon the severity of the communication impairment. The primary objective for every patient must be to restore communication to a functional level. "Functional" varies widely depending upon the level of disability of the individual patient.

For the severely involved patient, functional communication might be:

1. To respond consistently to "yes–no" questions by nodding the head, blinking the eyes, or squeezing the hand.
2. To point to needs on a picture communication board or in a picture communication booklet.

For higher-level patients, functional communication goals might include:

1. To restore verbal communication to a functional level by improving word retrieval (aphasia).
2. To increase intelligibility of speech by slowing down rate of speaking (dysarthria).
3. To increase intelligibility of speech through oral muscle exercises (dysarthria).
4. To restore verbal communication to a functional level by reestablishing control over articulatory movements and sequencing of sounds (apraxia).
5. To improve writing/spelling to a functional level to augment verbal communication (aphasia, dysarthria, and apraxia).
6. To restore reading to a functional level (aphasia, dysarthria, and apraxia).

If the speech–language pathologist works with dysphagic patients, the goals will include mastery of appropriate oral muscle exercises, positioning, and a hierarchy of liquids and foods that the patient will learn how to swallow safely.

Occasionally, the speech–language pathologist has the opportunity to intervene briefly with terminally ill patients or those with progressive degenerative conditions. In a "hospice-type" situation, the goals are not rehabilitative in nature but are geared toward preserving function for as long as possible. Goals for these patients might be to maintain use of verbal communication by muscle exercises, to prescribe and teach patients how to use assistive devices or augmentative communication systems when verbal communication is no longer possible.

Appropriate, attainable, and measurable goals must be established as a result of the diagnostic testing.

The patient's responses to the test items during the diagnostic session will give the therapist important cues to what will be the most appropriate methods and techniques to use during therapy. The disabilities discovered tell the therapist what to work on; the abilities discovered tell the therapist how to remediate the disabilities. For example, many patients have difficulty recalling or retrieving the names of objects, but they can say them readily in a sentence-completion format ("You shave with a ____") or when they see the written word (*razor*). If the patient responds best to the sentence-completion format, then the therapist knows to rely heavily on sentence-completion tasks in the early stages of treatment. If the patient responds best to a written word cue, then therapy should begin with matching written words to objects and pictures in the patient's environment. Other patients may be able to produce words most easily when the therapist gives an initial sound or syllable cue. It is the responsibility of the therapist during the diagnostic session to determine how the patient responds best and to use the patient's strong suit for planning the most appropriate methods and techniques to use during therapy.

An important but somewhat difficult aspect of the diagnostic session is determining the prognosis for improvement, referred to as the *rehabilitation potential*. This is important because insurance companies do not want home health agency personnel working with patients who have limited potential for recovering functional communication skills. Determining rehabilitation potential is difficult because there are so many factors that must be considered, and many of these factors do not have clear-cut predictors. Patients have been known to fool us and show remarkable improvement in the face of seemingly insurmountable odds. Several key factors related to prognosis include:

### SITE OF LESION

Advances in medical technology have made it possible for the neurologist to determine precisely where in the brain the insult occurred. CT scans (Computed Tomography) and MRI (Magnetic Resonance Imaging) pinpoint both the site and the extent of the lesion. Research in speech–language pathology, radiology, and neurology is currently developing ways to predict the type and degree of impairment and the prognosis for recovery based on site-of-lesion information. The more specific and localized the damaged area, the better the prognosis for improvement. A generalized or widespread area of damage has a less favorable prognosis.

### TIME SINCE CVA

Immediately following a hemorrhage or embolism, the damage appears to be more extensive than it actually is. There may be temporary paralysis to one or both sides of the body and a total inability to utter any sounds. Fortunately, there is a period of rapid recovery, known as *spontaneous recovery*, when the brain begins to heal itself. As blood is reabsorbed from surrounding tissue, function begins to return as a result of this healing process. Traditionally, the patient spent much of this crucial recovery time in the acute-care hospital. The trend in recent years, since the advent of DRGs and "managed care," is that more patients are being discharged from the hospital to their home or a nursing home while they are still "acute-care" patients. It is important for the speech–language pathologist evaluating a patient in a hospital, nursing home, or home health setting to know how much time has elapsed since the CVA. Although early intervention can be crucial to the patient's eventual recovery, the primary role in early intervention must be one of counseling with the patient and family rather than "working with the patient." It is not possible to do a thorough and valid evaluation on a patient who is still in the acute stage. You can quickly assess the patient's present level of functioning, but what you are actually measuring is his ability to respond to a test-taking situation at a time when he is far more concerned about life–death and survival. You cannot adequately or accurately assess the patient's abilities and disabilities, formulate a plan of treatment, establish appropriate goals, or determine prognosis for eventual recovery until the patient has at least stabilized medically, which frequently includes several changes in type and dosage of medication.

This does not imply that there is not a significant role for the speech–language pathologist in the acute-care hospital. There is never a time when the patient and the family are more in need of a kind, gentle, and understanding professional than immediately after a CVA. The hospital speech–language pathologist can fulfill that need by providing information, supportive counseling, and an early method of communication to the patient and his family. Rehabilitation efforts should begin as soon as possible, within a few days of the CVA; however, it will be 2 to 3 weeks post-CVA, or after awakening for comatose patients, before a valid assessment can be made regarding the patient's residual abilities, disabilities, and prognosis.

The warning to the home health speech–language pathologist is that the patient may not yet be medically stable, pharmacologically stable, or through the initial spontaneous recovery period when the initial diagnostic session is done. This should be considered especially if the patient is minimally responsive and appears to have a very limited prognosis. If the patient has not had sufficient time for early recovery, it is advisable to initiate "trial" therapy or to reevaluate in a few weeks, rather than hastily dismiss the patient's chances for significant recovery.

## RECOVERY SINCE CVA

A very important aspect of the patient's present status and eventual recovery is how severely he was affected immediately after the stroke and how much he has already regained. It is important to ask the family and the patient the following questions. Could he communicate with you or the doctors after the stroke? How did he communicate? How does he communicate now? It is also helpful to get as much medical information as possible regarding the patient's admission, course of treatment, and hospital discharge.

## COMPLICATING MEDICAL CONDITIONS

Prognosis for recovery of communication abilities is affected by other medical complications which must be assessed. Among the factors that can impede progress are: history of previous strokes, poor hearing, poor vision, and chronic medical conditions such as diabetes, arthritis, and heart disease. These chronic medical conditions require separate medications that may affect the patient's energy and motivation. It is important for the rehabilitation specialists to know as much as possible about the patient's medical history and current status. If the patient has had previous strokes, the therapists need to know what impairments are the result of the current CVA and what impairments are residual effects from previous strokes. If the patient has visual or auditory acuity deficits, the type of activities and materials used in therapy procedures will have to be modified. If the patient wears glasses, hearing aids, or dentures, these assistive devices should be worn during the diagnostic and treatment sessions. This will appear obvious to the medical professionals but it has never occurred to some patients or family members that Grandma needs her glasses or hearing aids, so be sure to ask. Be alert especially for changes in vision which may have occurred as a result of the CVA.

## PATIENT'S ATTITUDE

Perhaps the most important factor in determining prognosis for eventual recovery is the patient himself. As with several of the other factors discussed, patient attitude can be better determined several weeks after the CVA than immediately post-CVA. Almost without exception, patients experience periods of depression and feelings of loss of dignity and self-worth because of the devastating circumstances of the stroke. The individual's responses to these circumstances, however, reflect their attitudes toward life and greatly affect their prognosis for recovery. Goals must be realistic but the patient MUST have goals.

### FAMILY ATTITUDE

One of the most difficult prognostic factors to evaluate accurately is the attitude of the most crucial caregivers — the patient's immediate family. It is very easy to identify the two extremes — those who do not seem to care enough and those who seem to care too much. However, the majority of our patients will be a part of a family "in-between." Family counseling is a vital part of the rehabilitation process. The patient with the best prognosis for eventual recovery has a supportive, sympathetic, but somewhat assertive family. Just as the patient's pre-CVA attitude toward life affects her eventual recovery, the family's pre-CVA attitude toward the patient and toward life in general affects their post-CVA attitudes.

### THE PATIENT'S AGE AND PRE-CVA CONDITION

Age may be a significant factor in prognosis. The younger the patient is when the CVA occurs, the better the prognosis for recovery. There appear to be more people having strokes in their 30s, 40s, and 50s recently, and, as a rule, these younger patients seem to recover better than patients in their 60s, 70s, and 80s. The exceptions are the chronically ill younger patients who have medical histories including diabetes, heart disease, or other debilitating medical complications. Quite possibly, these other conditions and the medications necessary to treat them have ravaged the brain and body, or have dampened the will to "get well." Younger healthier tissue can respond more readily to rehabilitation efforts. There is also a stronger motivation for the younger patient to "get back to normal" as quickly as possible. "Back to normal" for young patients often means resuming job responsibilities, raising a family, and resuming cooking and household chores. There are more demands, internally and externally, for the younger patient to recover. These factors, coupled with the resiliency of youth, yield a better prognosis for recovery for the younger stroke patient.

# COUNSELING THE PATIENT AND FAMILY

An important part of the initial diagnostic session is interpreting for the patient and family members the results of the testing you have just completed. Many of the best test batteries require a significant amount of time and effort to interpret and score the data to develop profiles; yet you should be able to summarize, in layman's terms, what you have discerned as the patient's abilities and disabilities. The strengths need to be pointed out to the patient and her family with suggestions for daily activities that utilize those strengths. The weaknesses need to be discussed candidly, in terms of how those specific deficits impact daily living.

Concrete suggestions for facilitating daily communication need to be made before leaving the patient's home. It is not acceptable to go into a patient's home, test the patient, and leave with the promise that you'll be back next week to start therapy. "Therapy" started when you walked in the door, not as an aftermath of diagnosis. If the patient is nonverbal, you should leave a basic communication board with a quick demonstration to the family of how to use it. If the patient is minimally verbal, you should begin the process of teaching the family how to facilitate verbal responses. This involves counseling the family on how to avoid asking open-ended questions such as, "What do you want for breakfast?" If the patient can respond only by shaking her head "yes" or "no," the family needs to be taught to ask, "Do you want cereal?" If the patient can respond verbally with minimal cueing, the caregiver can be taught to ask multiple-choice questions: "Do you want bacon or sausage?" In this format, the pattern for response is fresh in the patient's mind, and she should be able to answer verbally. If this does not elicit the answer, then the caregiver should utilize "yes–no" questions (i.e., "Do you want bacon?"). This type of facilitation can be explained briefly to the family immediately after the testing has been completed and needs to be accomplished at that initial session.

Counseling of this type involves the family in the rehabilitation process from the beginning. Regardless of the type of setting in which you see the patient and regardless of the patient's communication deficit, "therapy" is not something you do to the patient, but it is something you teach the patient and the family to actively participate in. With a few exceptions of wealthy and famous people (Patricia Neal, Joseph Kennedy Sr.), who were able to hire full-time, live-in, 24-hour-a-day speech–language pathologists and physical therapists, what we are able to accomplish in two or three visits a week pales in comparison to what cooperative trained family members can accomplish. We must teach them what they need to know to become effective communication facilitators.

It is important to summarize briefly for the patient and family how the treatment will proceed and the anticipated course of recovery. There are usually constraints placed by third-party payers on the length and amount of therapy that can be provided. By explaining to the patient and family from the beginning the limits on our ability to continue services indefinitely, we can also stress the importance of family participation in the therapy process.

The final area to be covered during the initial visit is setting up a schedule for subsequent treatment visits. Because of travel time and location of the patient's home, there is less flexibility in scheduling visits than in hospital, nursing home, or outpatient rehabilitation facilities. The days for the visits may be determined by which days you will be in that part of the city, county, or state. If other services are involved, the speech–language pathologist will need to coordinate her schedule with physical therapy, occupational therapy, home health aides, nurses, and any other professionals who might be involved. It is never ideal to see the patient after PT due to fatigue or while the aide is changing the bed or bathing the patient. Some patients respond better at certain times of the day, and, whenever possible, the speech–language pathologist should try to schedule therapy at the time of day when the patient is most responsive. Another consideration that should not be a factor, but occasionally presents a problem, is scheduling therapy that conflicts with the patient's or caregiver's TV preferences. Some people are devoted to watching certain game shows, talk shows, or soap operas on a daily basis, and either the patient or caregiver may resent therapy if it is scheduled at certain times. In the home health setting, the primary caregiver often has little if any respite from taking care of the needs of the patient. Avoid scheduling therapy at a time that would interfere with what limited diversions the caregiver might maintain, like a weekly beauty parlor appointment, bridge club, sporting event, or church group. These outings are important to the family, as they attempt to cope with the patient's illness.

# TESTING PROCEDURES

Rosenbek *et al.* (1989) differentiate between appraisal and diagnosis. They define *appraisal* as the data collected and analyzed by the clinician, and *diagnosis* as the labeling of the patient's communication disorder.

Appraisal is based on information obtained from three sources: the patient's biography, medical and neurological examination results, and performance on tests administered by the rehabilitation specialists.

The biographical data should include:

> the patient's name and what he or she likes to be called, address, place of birth, date of birth, education, date of onset of brain damage, premorbid and present handedness, racial/ethnic group, previous and present marital status, occupational status at onset and at present, highest occupational level attained, estimate of premorbid communicativeness, estimate of premorbid intelligence, premorbid languages used and an estimate of their usage, present environment, number and kinds of people in the present environment, past and present interests and hobbies, and how the patient currently spends his or her day. (p. 56)

Medical and neurological information should be obtained from the patient's physician and the medical records. Rosenbek *et al.* (1989) summarize pertinent medical data in Figure 3.

Behavioral data encompasses the patient's performance on tests administered by the speech–language pathologist, as well as the physical therapist, occupational therapist, neurologist, physiatrist, and any other professionals who are involved in the management of the patient.

There are a number of diagnostic tests available to the speech–language pathologist, with additional protocols being developed, researched, published, and marketed on a continuing basis. It is difficult for the practicing clinician to be familiar with every possible diagnostic test available. The wide variety and degree of impairments demonstrated by patients require that the speech–language pathologist utilize a diversity of testing procedures.

Spreen and Risser (1991) give an excellent critique of many of the tests that are currently available to the speech–language pathologist. Figure 4 summarizes the different types of tests that are frequently used for appraisal of the neurologically impaired patient.

Rosenbek *et al.* (1989) recommend that an appraisal battery include a measure of general language ability, a motor speech evaluation, and an assessment of the patient's orientation and fund of general information. They state that

> evaluating motor speech indicates the presence or absence of coexisting apraxia of speech and/or dysarthria. The general language measure provides an overall impression of severity, strengths, and weaknesses in each modality, and suggestions for further exploration with specific modality measures. Appraising orientation and fund of general information assist in deciding whether what we are seeing is aphasia, confusion, or dementia. (p. 77)

Figure 3 –
**Medical Data
Collected to Assist
Managing Patients
Suspected of
Suffering Aphasia.**

Reprinted with permission
from Rosenbek *et al.* (1989).

| Variable | Measures |
|---|---|
| Vision | Acuity, corrected and uncorrected; field abnormalities |
| Hearing | Acuity aided and unaided; discrimination; ear pathologies |
| Limb involvement | Upper and lower; spasticity, weakness, coordination |
| Brain stem signs | Facial weakness, facial sensory loss; nystagmus, extraocular movement (EOM) and/or gaze impairment; dysphagia; other bulbar signs |
| Etiology | Type (CVA, trauma, infection, etc.); date of onset |
| Previous CNS involvement | Type; date of onset |
| Localization of brain damage | Hemisphere and lobe or lobes for current episode and any previous episode; source (clinical, CT, PETT, MRI, etc.) |
| Specific, complete diagnosis | For example, thrombosis of left middle cerebral artery, with right hemiparesis, hemisensory defect, hemianopsia, and expressive aphasia |
| Other major medical diagnoses | For example, diabetes, chronic cardiac arrhythmia |
| Medications | Number, types, and side effects |

**Figure 4 –
Summary of Tests
Available.**

## Summary of Tests Available

### TESTS FOR MOTOR SPEECH EVALUATION

1. Apraxia Battery for Adults (Dabul, 1979).
2. Motor Speech Evaluation (Wertz *et al.*, 1991).
3. Frenchay Dysarthria Assessment (Enderby, 1983).
4. Assessment of Intelligibility of Dysarthric Speech (Yorkston and Beukelman, 1981).

### GENERAL LANGUAGE MEASURES: COMPREHENSIVE APHASIA TESTS

1. Boston Diagnostic Aphasia Evaluation (Goodglass and Kaplan, 1983a).
2. Western Aphasia Battery (Kertesz, 1982).
3. Minnesota Test for Differential Diagnosis of Aphasia (Schuell, 1965).
4. Porch Index of Communicative Abilities (Porch, 1967).

### SCREENING TESTS FOR APHASIA

1. Bedside Evaluation and Screening Test for Aphasia (Fitch-West and Sands, 1987).
2. Aphasia Language Performance Scales (Keenan and Brassell, 1975).

### SPECIFIC MODALITY TESTS

**Auditory Comprehension**

1. Token Test (DeRenzi and Vignolo, 1962).
2. Revised Token Test (McNeil and Prescott, 1978).
3. Auditory Comprehension Test for Sentences (Shewan, 1979).
4. Functional Auditory Comprehension Task (LaPointe and Horner, 1978).

**Reading**

1. Reading Comprehension Battery for Aphasia (LaPointe and Horner, 1979).

**Oral Expressive Language**

1. Reporter's Test (DeRenzi and Ferrari, 1978).
2. Boston Naming Test (Kaplan, Goodglass, and Weintraub, 1983).

**Gesture**

1. New England Pantomime Tests (Duffy and Duffy, 1984).

### FUNCTIONAL COMMUNICATION TESTS

1. Communicative Abilities in Daily Living (Holland, 1980).
2. Functional Communication Profile (Sarno, 1969).
3. Functional Assessment of Communication Skills for Adults (ASHA–FACS) (Frattali *et al.*, 1995).

In the home health setting, the therapist does not have the luxury of extensive diagnostic testing. It is recommended that one of the aphasia screening tests or parts of a comprehensive aphasia battery be administered initially to direct the therapist to other types of testing that might be necessary. While administering the "aphasia" test, the examiner must be alert to possible interferences from motor speech disorders or generalized dementia. When indicated, further probing must be done.

The home health speech–language pathologist should be familiar with the following textbooks:

> *Diagnosis and Evaluation in Speech Pathology*, 5th ed., by W. Haynes and R. Pindzola (Allyn and Bacon, Needham Heights, MA, 1998).
>
> *Medical Speech–Language Pathology: A Practitioner's Guide*, by A. Johnson and B. Jacobson (Thieme Medical Publishers, New York, 1998).
>
> *Sourcebook for Medical Speech Pathology*, by L. A. Golper (Singular Publishing Group, San Diego, 1992).

The Porch Index of Communicative Abilities (PICA) test format can be modified and used with home health patients. The *Modified PICA* is administered and scored according to PICA guidelines; however, it utilizes five objects rather than ten, for the convenience of balancing test items on a pillow for bedridden patients. It is possible to assess a patient's communicative abilities and disabilities, strengths and weaknesses, differentiate between the components of receptive aphasia, expressive aphasia, apraxia, dysarthria, dementia, and/or cognitive deficits on the basis of a "modified" five-item PICA. Further testing can be done in any problem areas identified.

# PIERCE LANGUAGE SCREENING BATTERY

Higher-level patients can be evaluated using the Pierce Language Screening Battery (see Figure 5).

**Figure 5**
**Pierce Language**
**Screening Battery.**

Patient:                  Medical Record #

Date:

1. Proverbs:

Don't count your chickens _____

I'll cross that bridge _____

A penny saved _____

Don't kill the goose that _____

A bird in the hand _____

The grass is always greener _____

Don't cry over _____

You can't have your cake _____

Don't put all your eggs _____

People who live in glass houses _____

2. Brand Names:

| | |
|---|---|
| Maxwell House: | Eveready: |
| Kodak: | Lipton: |
| Purina: | Maytag: |
| Delta: | Winston: |
| McDonald's: | Peter Pan: |

3. Famous People:

| | |
|---|---|
| Lucille Ball _____ | Ann Landers _____ |
| Elvis Presley _____ | Abraham Lincoln _____ |
| Bill Clinton _____ | Willie Mays _____ |
| Joe Namath _____ | Martin Luther King Jr. _____ |
| Liberace _____ | Lee Harvey Oswald _____ |

4. City/State:

| | |
|---|---|
| Memphis _____ | Dallas _____ |
| Chicago _____ | Seattle _____ |
| San Francisco _____ | Baltimore _____ |
| Orlando _____ | Las Vegas _____ |
| Tucson _____ | Omaha _____ |

5. Consequences: What would happen if?

You drop a glass on the floor?

You come up behind someone and say "BOO"?

You touch a hot stove?

You wear a pair of pants that are too big for you?

Your dog gets in a fight with a skunk?

Pierce Language Screening Battery

| Scoring Summary | Initial Evaluation | | Retest | Date: |
|---|---|---|---|---|
| 1. Proverbs | ___/10 = | % | ___/10 = | % |
| 2. Brand Names | ___/10 = | % | ___/10 = | % |
| 3. Famous People | ___/10 = | % | ___/10 = | % |
| 4. City/State | ___/10 = | % | ___/10 = | % |
| 5. Consequences | ___/5 = | % | ___/5 = | % |

# *Documentation*

# Chapter 4

# Documentation

## INTRODUCTION

The speech–language pathologist is responsible for writing an initial evaluation report, daily treatment notes, and a discharge summary report.

Specific requirements for documentation vary with each individual home health agency because regulations vary from state to state and from provider to provider. All documentation requirements are based on Medicare guidelines, which also change periodically. The HHA manual, *HCFA Publication 11*, provides the coverage criteria for physical, occupational, and speech therapy services as follows:

1. The skills of a qualified therapist are required due to the complexity of the service or the patient's condition.

2. The services must be reasonable and necessary to the patient's condition, that is, services provided must be consistent with the patient's needs, the problem itself, and the severity of the problem, and the amount, frequency and duration must be reasonable. The services must also be within accepted standards of medical practice.

3. The diagnosis and prognosis alone do not dictate coverage. A key issue is whether the skills of a therapist are needed to treat the patient's illness or injury.

4. There must be an expectation that the patient will make significant gains within a reasonable amount of time and/or the services are needed to set up a safe and effective maintenance program.

5. Teaching and training the patient, family, and caregiver may be covered if it is reasonable and necessary to the treatment of the patient's illness or injury.

Documentation at the time of the initial evaluation and in daily progress notes needs to be stated in OBJECTIVE terms, as much as possible. This often means reporting percentage of correct responses (e.g., 40% prompt and accurate, 85% accurate with delays).

In most home health agencies, the nursing staff has the major responsibility for ensuring that the patient's chart contain all the information required by the fiscal intermediary. The speech–language pathologist should be aware of the requirements, specifically as they relate to speech pathology services.

HCFA-485 is the Home Health Certification and Plan of Treatment. This form is completed by the nurse who admits or is assigned as Case Manager and MUST be signed by the referring physician. The plan of treatment states specifically what services will be provided to the patient, how often, and for how long. For example:

1. Home health aide 3xWKx4 (three times per week for 4 weeks) and 2xWKx5 (two times per week for 5 weeks) to assist the patient with bath and personal care.

2. RN for skilled nursing care 2xWKx6 (two times per week for 6 weeks) and 1xWKx3 (one time per week for 3 weeks) to monitor reactions to medication, vital signs, and for patient/caregiver training.

3. Speech–language pathologist 2xWKx9 (two times per week for 9 weeks) to improve oral muscle function for eating and communicating.

HCFA-486 is the Medical Update and Patient Information form. This is used for recertification, if and when additional treatment is needed beyond the initial 9-week certification period. Copies of HCFA-485 and-486 are included in the Appendix.

Information on each patient should be presented and discussed at Team Conferences attended by all agency personnel working with that patient (e.g., RN, home health aide, PT, OT, SLP, MSW). At the case conference, each discipline reports briefly on the goals, treatment activities, and progress of the patient. This provides an excellent opportunity for team collaboration and for interdisciplinary referrals. It also alerts the Case Manager to begin the recertification process several weeks before the current orders expire. Team conferences are documented and a summary report is placed in the patient's chart.

# INFORMATION THAT *MUST* BE IN THE PATIENT'S CHART

**Bill of Rights**. HCFA requires that the Patient's Bill of Rights be explained to the patient and caregiver. The patient and caregiver must acknowledge by their signatures that they have received this information.

**Advance Medical Directives**. Individual state laws vary regarding Advance Medical Directive and durable power of attorney, but HCFA requires that the chart document the patient's or legal guardian's wishes regarding whether or not the patient wishes "Do Not Resuscitate," organ donation, request or refusal of life support systems, and so on.

**DME and Supplies**. The plan of treatment lists all durable medical equipment (DME) and supplies already in the home and documents the need for any additional medical equipment and supplies. Documentation must show that the equipment and supplies are reasonable and necessary for the patient's treatment and recovery. To be reimbursed, DME and supplies must be ordered by the physician.

**Home Health Aide Supervision**. The nurse usually supervises the home health aide. If skilled nursing care is not required for a patient, the PT, OT, or SLP may need to document supervision of the home health aide, which is required every fourteen days. Individual home health agencies have developed different forms to use. The professional completing the form asks the patient/caregiver if the home health aide is fulfilling assigned tasks satisfactorily and states that home health aide services need to be continued.

# DOCUMENTATION REQUIREMENTS

1. Document the problem and date of onset.
2. Document the patient's level of functioning before the problem occurred.
3. Document the patient's level of functioning at the time of the initial assessment.
4. Document the patient's progress or lack of progress in the medical record in objective, comparative terms.
5. If the patient is not making progress or is regressing, document possible reasons, that is, hospitalization, exacerbation of conditions, etc.
6. Document testing when applicable.
7. Document changes to the Plan of Treatment, such as increase or decrease in the frequency of visits.

# TIPS ON DOCUMENTATION

1. **Write legibly**. Other staff members and reviewers must be able to read the information in the patient's chart.
2. **Use permanent black ink**. To correct an error, draw a line through the erroneous entry and initial it. Do not scratch out or "White-out" any information in the chart.

3. **For every entry, identify the date.** Times, if used, should be stated in "military time." Sign every entry with your name and title.

4. **Write chart notes in consecutive and chronological order**, with no skipped lines or gaps.

5. **Write daily visit notes either at the patient's home or as soon as possible after treatment is provided.**

6. **Be sure the patient's name and medical record number are correct** on the daily notes and on any forms in the chart.

# SPECIALIZED DOCUMENTATION REQUIREMENTS FOR DYSPHAGIA

The Medicare Manual lists specific criteria that must be met for the patient to qualify for speech pathology services for dysphagia. For patients with disorders of the oral, pharyngeal, or esophageal phase of swallowing, document the patient's level of alertness, motivation, cognition, and deglutition. For payment, at least one of the following conditions must be documented:

1. **History of aspiration problems, aspiration pneumonia, or risk for aspiration.** Possible problems to note include: nasal regurgitation, choking, frequent coughing up food or liquid during swallowing, wet or gurgly voice quality after swallow, delayed or slow swallow reflex.

2. **Presence of oral motor impairments**, such as drooling, "pocketing" or retaining food in the mouth, leakage of food or liquid placed in the mouth.

3. **Impaired salivary gland performance** and/or **presence of structural lesions in the pharynx** resulting in oropharyngeal swallowing difficulties.

4. **Incoordination, loss of sensation, or other neuromotor disturbances** that affect the patient's ability to bite, chew, form a bolus, and propel the bolus into the upper pharynx while protecting the airway.

5. **Post-surgical deficits** affecting the patient's ability to use oropharyngeal structures.

6. **Significant weight loss** directly related to non-oral nutrition (NG tube or G-tube feeding) and negative reaction to textures and consistencies.

7. **Existence of other conditions** such as presence of tracheostomy tube, reduced or inadequate laryngeal elevation, inadequate lip closure, inadequate velopharyngeal closure, or cricopharyngeal dysfunction.

# THE DIAGNOSTIC REPORT

Following the evaluation procedures, the speech–language pathologist needs to write a clear concise report. This report is intended for the referring physician, the home health agency, and the third party payer. Although it is appropriate for the report to contain some *technical terminology*, it is preferable to keep the information as *generic* as possible.

The diagnostic report establishes the baseline data necessary for assessing rehabilitation potential, setting realistic goals, and measuring communication status at periodic intervals. The diagnostic report should include a brief statement of pertinent medical history, a listing of tests administered (standardized or nonstandardized), a summary and interpretation of test results, and a statement of the diagnosis and severity of speech and language deficits. The report should conclude with the therapist's recommendations for frequency and duration of therapy, the treatment plan, the goals for treatment, and a statement of "rehabilitation potential."

Several examples of diagnostic reports appear on the following pages.

# Home Health, Inc.

## Paramedical Evaluation & Care Plan

To _____     Patient _____

From _____     Medical Record # _____

Date _____

———— was seen in his home for a speech and language evaluation on August 27, 20XX. Medical history includes a CVA on August 10, 20XX. Patient has diabetes. He was unable to talk following the CVA but appears to be regaining communication skills. Family reports that he has difficulty saying words and becomes frustrated when he tries to talk.

Formal and informal tests of language ability and cognitive functioning were utilized during the evaluation. A modification of the Porch Index of Communicative Abilities (using 5 items instead of 10) was administered with the following results:

Patient was able to point to objects and pictures by name and by function promptly and accurately. He could match identical objects and pictures to objects promptly and accurately. Verbal responses, such as naming objects, describing the objects, and sentence-completion tasks, were significantly delayed and occasionally off-target ("spoon" for "fork"). He often described the object in an attempt to cue himself in word retrieval. He was able to read and match written word cards to objects but reports difficulty comprehending text such as newspaper or magazine articles. Spelling and writing are basically intact at the one word level.

It is recommended that ———— be seen in his home for speech–language pathology services twice a week for 9 weeks. The goal of treatment will be to reduce word retrieval difficulties (i.e., expressive aphasia). Treatment will include counseling the family regarding facilitation techniques and teaching the patient to use compensatory strategies. Rehab. potential appears to be good.

_____          _____
Physician's Signature                 Speech–Language Pathologist

# Home Health, Inc.

## Paramedical Evaluation & Care Plan

To _____          Patient _____

From _____        Medical Record # _____

Date _____


—— was seen in her home for a speech and language evaluation on December 10, 20XX. She has a history of high blood pressure and suffered her third CVA two weeks ago. Until that event, Mrs. —— needed assistance with ADLs and used a walker, but speech and language were not affected by previous CVAs.

A modification of the PICA (using 5 items instead of 10) was administered. Tests results indicated no receptive aphasia. Speech intelligibility was so poor that it was difficult to assess expressive aphasia. Additional activities of picture naming and sentence completion ruled out any substantial degree of expressive aphasia. Items from the Apraxia Battery for Adults were attempted but were too frustrating for ——. Using a mirror, she was able to imitate tongue, lip, and jaw movements; however, range of motion was decreased. Analysis of muscle function during speech revealed that she is not moving her tongue, lips, and mandible adequately. There is some drooling from the right side of her mouth. The oral/facial muscle involvement is also affecting her eating/drinking. She is eating soft foods, taking small bites or sips, and holding her lips closed with her finger.

—— has no significant receptive or expressive aphasia, undetermined oral/verbal apraxia, and moderate dysarthria resulting from her recent CVA.

It is recommended that —— be seen for speech–language pathology services twice a week for 9 weeks. The goals for treatment will be: (1) to increase mobility and tonicity of the oral-facial muscles, and (2) to improve intelligibility of speech. Rehab potential appears to be good.


_____          _____
Physician's Signature            Speech–Language Pathologist

# Home Health, Inc.

## Paramedical Evaluation & Care Plan

To _____          Patient _____
From _____          Medical Record # _____
Date _____

_____ was seen in her daughter's home for a speech and language evaluation on October 23, 20XX. She was recently hospitalized (10/12/20XX through 10/18/20XX) with a CVA that resulted in expressive aphasia, according to the family.

_____ could not be aroused for any testing procedures. There was a noticeable change in her breathing pattern when I spoke to her or touched her arm, but she did not open her eyes, make any sounds, or follow any commands. The nurse reports that occasionally _____ opens her eyes briefly, squeezes someone's hand, and eats a little baby food or liquid from a syringe, but that she mostly sleeps. The nurse also reports that there have been several similar episodes in the past year when _____ appears to lapse into a coma; however, she usually "rallies" in a few days and becomes responsive.

Speech pathology intervention is not recommended at the present time because of the patient's low level of responses. She should be reevaluated if her condition improves. A picture communication board was left for the family to use as _____ recovers. The family was given a list of mechanically soft foods to feed Mrs. _____ instead of baby food.

_____          _____
Physician's Signature          Speech–Language Pathologist

# Home Health, Inc.

## Paramedical Evaluation & Care Plan

To _____          Patient _____

From _____          Medical Record # _____

Date _____

Speech–language evaluation, oral muscle examination, and swallowing evaluation were completed on ——— on July 11, 20XX. ——— was diagnosed with Parkinson's Disease approximately 1 year ago. She was hospitalized 2 weeks ago with toxemia resulting from her medication and is currently not taking any medication. This has caused an exacerbation of her symptoms.

The patient was alert and cooperative throughout the evaluation procedures. Results are summarized as follows:

1. **Speech**. Patient uses a very rapid rate of speaking, does not project voice, uses restricted movement of articulators, especially mandible and lips.

2. **Language**. Screening revealed no apparent receptive or expressive aphasia. Patient was able to respond correctly to all items on the Pierce Language Screening Battery.

3. **Oral Muscle Evaluation**. Decreased strength and range of movement in jaw muscles and lip muscles. Slight tremor in tongue on protrusion and lateralization but patient does not believe tongue tremors interfere with speaking or eating.

4. **Swallowing Evaluation**. Patient reports problems with the Oral Phase: (1) unable to open mouth wide enough to get food in, (2) unable to close lips while chewing, therefore uses fingers to push food back into her mouth, (3) unable to drink from a glass because the liquid leaks out the sides of her mouth. She has experienced no problems with choking or strangling on foods or liquids.

It was recommended that ——— be seen for speech–language pathology services twice a week for 9 weeks. The goals for treatment will be: (1) to slow down rate of speaking, (2) to increase breath support, and (3) to improve strength and range of movement of the jaw and lip muscles.

Rehab potential is good for goals as stated.

_____          _____
Physician's Signature              Speech–Language Pathologist

# Home Health, Inc.

## Paramedical Evaluation & Care Plan

To _____          Patient _____

From _____        Medical Record # _____

Date _____

———— was seen in her home for a speech and language evaluation on August 29, 20XX. She had a CVA approximately 1 week ago, which affected the left side of her body and her speech. She complains that her "words get tangled up."

The PICA Test for receptive and expressive aphasia was administered, with modifications necessitated by the patient's visual problems. She could identify and discuss the test items by holding them in her hand, but cannot see adequately enough to do any subtests requiring matching of pictures or written words. The testing was supplemented by numerous auditory–verbal tasks such as sentence completion, tell "what would happen if" and recalling of past events. ———— showed slight delays in her responses, but nothing that would indicate receptive or expressive aphasia. She was somewhat distracted by people and noises (telephone, doorbell, etc.) in the household.

Following the diagnostic evaluation, results and recommendations were explained to ———— and her daughter. Speech–language pathology is not recommended because I was unable to identify any problem areas that might be expected to improve as a result of therapy. I counseled with her and her daughter regarding: (1) the delays in response time — she will have to be patient with herself and give herself time to formulate her answers, and (2) the problems of communicating in a crowd — she can handle conversations one-on-one, but gets confused when several people are talking at once. I explained these as natural phenomena of advancing age, complicated by the CVA, but I anticipate that there will be some improvement as she recovers physically from the stroke. Mrs. ———— should be reevaluated in the future if there is a significant change in her verbal status.


_____          _____
Physician's Signature              Speech–Language Pathologist

# Home Health, Inc.

## Paramedical Evaluation & Care Plan

To _____        Patient _____

From _____        Medical Record # _____

Date _____

_____
_____
_____
_____
_____
_____
_____
_____
_____
_____
_____
_____
_____
_____
_____
_____
_____
_____
_____
_____
_____
_____
_____
_____
_____

_____        _____
Physician's Signature            Speech–Language Pathologist

# SOAP NOTES:
# DAILY TREATMENT NOTES

Some home health agencies require that treatment notes be stated in the format known as "SOAP notes." SOAP notes can be an accurate and efficient method of documenting all information pertinent to the visit. The SOAP outline is as follows:

**S**: SUBJECTIVE: Comments about patient/family.

**O**: OBJECTIVE: Treatment tasks or activities.

**A**: ASSESSMENT: How the patient is doing on treatment tasks.

**P**: PLAN: What therapist plans to do with patient in future visits.

*Example 1*

**S**: Pt seen in her home for Speech Pathology. Family reports she is talking more.

**O**: Treatment tasks included oral motor exercises for increasing tongue movements and lip closure. Pt needed mirror cueing for tongue movements to right side. Pt needed finger cueing to achieve lip closure.

**A**: Dysarthria persists but improving with oral exercises. Continue to practice 3x daily.

**P**: Continue ST 2x/wk. Encouraged pt and family to use mirror on table during meals.

*Example 2*

**S**: Pt lethargic today. Family reports he did not sleep well last night.

**O**: Reviewed sentence-completion tasks for body parts. 80% accurate but delayed on many responses. New: sentence completion for household objects. 60% prompt and accurate. Needed first phoneme cue for remainder. Practice daily.

**A**: Word retrieval is improving but still needs max cueing.

**P**: Continue with plan. Do TV Shows next.

# PROGRESS REPORTS

Approximately once a month, the daily treatment note should be written in the form of a Progress Report. The progress report should summarize the patient's response to treatment and document the need for continuing treatment. Whenever possible, test–retest information that reflects change should be included in the progress report. Monthly re-evaluation of patients enrolled in restorative speech pathology programs is considered part of the treatment session and cannot be billed as a separate evaluation for billing purposes.

# DISCHARGE SUMMARY REPORTS

At the conclusion of treatment, a discharge summary report is written and sent to the referring physician. Several examples of Discharge Summary Reports follow.

# Speech–Language Pathology Progress Notes

| **Patient:** | | **Medical Record #:** |
| --- | --- | --- |

4/13/XX      Discharge Summary

9:00            Mr. ——— has been seen in his home for Speech–Language Pathology three times per week since his initial evaluation on 12/10/20XX.

     Today, I readministered the Pierce Language Screening Battery to assess his progress and reevaluate the need for continuing speech pathology services. Results are summarized as follows:

| Subtest | 12/10/XX | 4/13/XX |
| --- | --- | --- |
| 1. Proverbs | 75% | 90% |
| 2. Brand Names | 40% | 90% |
| 3. Famous People | 50% | 80% |
| 4. City/State | 90% | 100% |
| 5. Consequences | 60% | 100% |

     Test/retest results were discussed with Mr. and Mrs. ——— and were related to specific activities we have covered during his therapy. They were encouraged to continue practicing daily on the papers in his "speech book." Both are aware of and appreciative of the significant progress he has made.

     Patient discharged with goals accomplished.

                                             **Signature**

# Speech–Language Pathology Progress Notes

| Patient: | Medical Record #: |
|---|---|

2/7/20XX     Discharge Summary

10:10     Mrs. ——— has been seen in her home for Speech–Language Pathology twice a week since her initial evaluation on 12/2/20XX. Readministered Modified PICA testing. Significant improvement! 80% of responses were prompt and accurate. Remainder were somewhat delayed but correct after she ~~to~~ took time to think through them. No perseveration. No neologisms. Pt is aware of and pleased with her progress. She complains of "fumbling" on her words occasionally, so we reviewed the strategies I've taught her to use when she experiences difficulty. Counseled her caregiver (niece) on techniques to facilitate word retrieval. She verbalizes that she is using what I've taught her in daily conversations with Mrs. ———.

Patient discharged with goals accomplished.

**Signature**

# Speech–Language Pathology Progress Notes

| *Patient:* | *Medical Record #:* |
|---|---|

5-23-XX    Last appointment — Discharge Summary

John ——— has been seen in his home for Speech–Language Pathology services 2x weekly since his initial evaluation on 3/29/20XX. He has moderate verbal apraxia with impairment of reading comprehension and spelling/writing. The goals for treatment were (1) to improve his ability to sequence sounds and syllables and (2) to improve short term memory.

Progress has been excellent throughout the treatment program. Mr. ——— and his wife are highly motivated and have followed through on all homework assignments and suggestions for incorporating therapy activities into daily living. He monitors his own speech very well and keeps trying until he gets it right. He still has mild apraxic difficulty.

I recommend continuing speech services and discussed the options with Mr. and Mrs. ——— at length. Pt's wife is currently in great pain from arthritis, and the family feels that he cannot maintain "homebound" status because he must take over her responsibilities for going to the grocery store, drug store, etc. We jointly agreed to DC Speech Pathology at this time, although I know he would benefit from continuing treatment. I provided them with sufficient activity pages and feel confident that they will continue practicing on assignments.

Pt discharged from therapy with goals accomplished. He has made significant improvement.

**Signature**

# Speech–Language Pathology Progress Notes

**Patient:**                                          **Medical Record #:**

# Counseling the Patient and Family

# Counseling the Patient and Family

## INTRODUCTION

The physical therapist, occupational therapist, and speech–language pathologist in the home health setting often must assume roles traditionally held by social workers and family counselors. Many therapists have not received any direct training in patient and family counseling. Some home health agencies do not have a social worker as a member of the patient care team. Nevertheless, counseling the patient and family is a vital part of the rehabilitative process.

This chapter will introduce the clinician to the types of problems most often encountered particularly with the adult neurologically involved patient. It is vital for the home health therapist to address the concerns of the patient and the caregivers.

The patient who can communicate is able to ask the doctors, nurses, and therapists a variety of questions about his condition, what caused it, and the anticipated prognosis for recovery. However, for the patient locked into silence or ineffective communication, these vitally important questions go unspoken and therefore unanswered. The perceptive therapist verbalizes for the patient the questions he would ask and provides the answers he is desperately seeking. Rehabilitation therapists can provide an important service to patients by acknowledging their concerns, fears, and bewilderment, even when we cannot provide all of the answers. These are some of the more common concerns of patients and caregivers.

# TRAUMATIC EFFECT OF SUDDEN ONSET

With the majority of medical maladies, the patient becomes ill, is diagnosed, receives treatment, and has a period of time to mentally and psychologically adjust to the disease process. Even the dreaded diseases, such as cancer, diabetes, and Alzheimer's, allow the patient and family time to read, study, question, and participate in decisions regarding treatment, and to prepare for the eventual outcome.

Heart attack, stroke, and head or spinal cord injury, on the other hand, usually strike without warning and are far more devastating to the patient and the family because they are robbed of the opportunity to plan for the occurrence. At one moment, the patient is a fully functioning child, adolescent, or adult. Suddenly and unpredictably, everything changes for both patient and family. To acknowledge the traumatic effect of sudden onset, this author frequently relates her experience of several years ago. Needing very minor surgery, she spent weeks preparing for a 3-day hospitalization and a 4-week recuperation at home. Preparations included extra grocery shopping, cooking and freezing meals for the family, carpool arrangements for school and soccer practices, and literally hundreds of similar details that allowed her to exercise some control over the situation. Precisely what the stroke patient or accident victim has lost is that sense of control. It helps to have someone at least verbalize and understand the devastating circumstance.

# FRUSTRATION OF INABILITY TO CARE FOR SELF

Following many surgical procedures and medical conditions, there is a period of time when the patient is unable to perform self-care tasks and the activities of daily living. It is very difficult for many patients to have to rely on others, family members and "strangers," to take care of basic bodily functions — bathing, toileting, and feeding — that the patient has done for himself all of his adult life. The loss of dignity and sense of self-worth can be as devastating to the patient as the incapacitation itself. During the patient's hospitalization, the nursing staff has handled administering to the patient's needs with skill and varying degrees of empathy. In the home, the untrained family members assume this responsibility. It is important that home health personnel give the family the support, counseling, and training they need to carry out these tasks. Much of this responsibility falls on the home health nursing staff; however, the rehabilitation therapists need to be aware of the patient's frustrations and the family's insecurities.

# FEARS OF HAVING TO DEPEND UPON OTHERS

Closely related to the patient's frustration at her inability to care for herself is the fear of having to depend upon others indefinitely. Many families face decisions regarding the need for nursing home care on a temporary or permanent basis. In their younger, healthier lives, they may have promised each other that they would never "commit" the beloved spouse or parent to a nursing home. So even thoughts of placement bring forth tremendous guilt and negative emotions. Patients have fears about whether or not they will be able to work again, to provide for themselves and their families, to resume *normal* activities. They do not know whether they will get better or worse. These fears need to be addressed, and often it is the home health care professional who is there to address them.

# ABUSE OF INFORMED CONSENT

To protect themselves against malpractice lawsuits, doctors and hospitals have gone overboard on explaining to the patient and family everything that could possibly go wrong as a result of each and every test and treatment procedure. They focus on the *worst-case scenario*. Therapists need to be aware that our patients and their families have been subjected to this negativism. While we do not want to foster unrealistic expectations, it is important to be as positive as possible toward the patient and family.

# LOSS OF COMPANIONSHIP: SHATTERED DREAMS

- The young person who sustains a traumatic brain injury may be abandoned by friends who are uncomfortable around him and busy pursuing their own lives and activities.
- The patient whose stroke makes communication difficult cannot talk with her family about daily activities.
- The spouse who must now assume responsibility for family matters must do so without seeking or receiving the advice and assistance of the patient.

Speech serves the purposes of allowing us to make our wants and needs known; it enables us to solve problems by discussing possible solutions. When speech is impaired, frustration and anger cannot be released in normal and socially acceptable ways.

The loss of communication, and thus of companionship, is perhaps a far greater loss than impairment of bodily functions.

# FINANCIAL CONCERNS

In this age of escalating health care costs, financial concerns plague many families. When illness or disease strikes a family member, there is the loss of future income-producing potential. It is a real shock to the patient to realize that he or she may not be able to go back to work. It is a shock to the spouse who may have to re-enter the job market after years of being a homemaker, or who may have to take time off from her job to care for her loved one. People in crisis situations need time and nurturing, and perhaps counseling, to come to grips with the financial aspects of long-term illness or incapacitation.

Health care costs and rehabilitation services are undeniably expensive. Usually, the patient and family have felt at least reasonably secure that private health insurance or Medicare would cover the bulk of the costs of medical treatment. It is not until after injury or illness occurs that people become aware that necessary equipment and services are denied or excluded from their coverage, or even that their deductibles and 20% copayments take a substantial chunk out of the family bank account.

Many families have saved money faithfully for their *golden years*, only to have their plans and dreams shattered by unanticipated medical costs. Although the home health therapists cannot solve these problems for their patients, it is important to acknowledge their existence and the effect on the patient and the family.

# PATIENT AND FAMILY EDUCATION

A significant aspect of patient and family counseling is patient and family education. Many of our patients are "medically naive." They DO NOT understand about stroke, traumatic brain injury, hospital procedures, CT scans, MRIs, medications, and a host of other things that have been thrust upon them. A portion of each treatment session should be devoted to patient and family education. This text provides information that the speech–language pathologist can copy and give to the patient and family.

# SUGGESTIONS FOR CAREGIVERS

Counseling and educating the patient and family must be part of EVERY treatment session. Figure 6, Suggestions for Caregivers (written in both male and female formats), should be discussed with the family either at the initial appointment or soon thereafter. They need to understand and begin to accept that the patient has changed and that they will need to change the way in which they relate to that family member.

---

**SUGGESTIONS FOR CAREGIVERS: MALE**

---

1. Speak to the patient in simple rather than complex sentences. Use adult vocabulary. Don't baby-talk.

2. Don't raise the volume of your voice or exaggerate lip movements. Speak naturally but slowly.

3. Give the patient time to respond. Repeat–rephrase.

4. Although a patient may not be able to use any expressive speech and seems unable to understand speech, he probably understands more than is apparent. Be cautious of remarks made in his presence.

5. Provide opportunities for the patient to speak and encourage him to ask for things he wants. Do not, however, force the patient if he does not want to try speech. Use facilitation techniques that make it easier for the patient to respond.

6. Avoid saying words for the patient, and try not to interrupt when he is trying to talk. Accept the speech attempts being made. However, if after several attempts he is unable to say the word, give him the word before he becomes frustrated.

7. The patient may have periods of crying or laughing for no apparent reason. Try not to react emotionally.

8. Swearing is an automatic response and comes out involuntarily. Try not to react to swearing with shock, anger, or amusement.

9. Encourage the use of social greetings such as hello, hi, goodbye, and thank you. These are also automatic responses and are usually easier for the patient to say.

10. Encourage the patient to write or print if at all possible. If a hemiplegia is present, have him use his good hand.

11. If no speech is possible, encourage the patient to use gestures. Ask him to describe with his hands or show you what he means.

12. Praise the patient for successful achievements regardless of how minor they may seem. Focus on the things he can do, not the things he can't do.

13. The patient may repeat words or actions over and over beyond meaning. This is known as *perseveration* and is very common. Try to break it by changing the stimulus or task.

14. Find and utilize humorous situations. Humor is a powerful ally provided it is not confused with ridicule.

15. Remember that the patient is an adult; treat him like one.

---

**Figure 6A
Suggestions for
Caregivers: Male.**

**SUGGESTIONS FOR CAREGIVERS: FEMALE**

1. Speak to the patient in simple rather than complex sentences. Use adult vocabulary. Don't baby-talk.

2. Don't raise the volume of your voice or exaggerate lip movements. Speak naturally but slowly.

3. Give the patient time to respond. Repeat—rephrase.

4. Although a patient may not be able to use any expressive speech and seems unable to understand speech, she probably understands more than is apparent. Be cautious of remarks made in her presence.

5. Provide opportunities for the patient to speak, and encourage her to ask for things she wants. Do not, however, force the patient if she does not want to try speech. Use facilitation techniques that make it easier for the patient to respond.

6. Avoid saying words for the patient and try not to interrupt when she is trying to talk. Accept the speech attempts being made. However, if after several attempts she is unable to say the word, give her the word before she becomes frustrated.

7. The patient may have periods of crying or laughing for no apparent reason. Try not to react emotionally.

8. Swearing is an automatic response and comes out involuntarily. Try not to react to swearing with shock, anger, or amusement.

9. Encourage the use of social greetings such as hello, hi, goodbye, and thank you. These are also automatic responses and are usually easier for the patient to say.

10. Encourage the patient to write or print if at all possible. If a hemiplegia is present, have her use her good hand.

11. If no speech is possible, encourage the patient to use gestures. Ask her to describe with her hands or show you what she means.

12. Praise the patient for successful achievements regardless of how minor they may seem. Focus on the things she can do, not the things she can't do.

13. The patient may repeat words or actions over and over beyond meaning. This is known as *perseveration* and is very common. Try to break it by changing the stimulus or task.

14. Find and utilize humorous situations. Humor is a powerful ally provided it is not confused with ridicule.

15. Remember that the patient is an adult; treat her like one.

**Figure 6B**
**Suggestions for Caregivers: Female.**

# USEFUL RESOURCES FOR PATIENT AND FAMILY COUNSELING AND PATIENT AND FAMILY EDUCATION

Ahn, J., and Ferguson, G. (1992). *Recovering from a Stroke* (Harper Paperbacks, New York).

Caplan, L. R., Dyken, M. L., and Easton, J. D. (1994). *American Heart Association Family Guide to Stroke Treatment, Recovery, and Prevention* (Times Books/Random House, New York).

Dikengil, A. (1994). *Communication Carryover for Adults* (Communication Skill Builders, Tucson).

Foyder, J. E. (1986). *Family Caregiver's Guide* (Kendall-Futuro, Cincinnati).

Johnstone, M. (1987). *Home Care for the Stroke Patient: Living in a Pattern* (Churchill-Livingstone, New York).

Jones, C., and Lorman, J. (1986a). *Aphasia: A Guide for the Patient and Family* (Interactive Therapeutics, Stow, OH).

Jones, C., and Lorman, J. (1986b). *Apraxia: A Guide for the Patient and Family* (Interactive Therapeutics, Stow, OH).

Jones, C., and Lorman, J. (1986c). *Dysarthria: A Guide for the Patient and Family* (Interactive Therapeutics, Stow, OH).

Jones, C., and Lorman, J. (1988). *Traumatic Brain Injury: A Guide for the Patient and Family* (Interactive Therapeutics, Stow, OH).

Knight, M. (1996). *Right Brain Stroke: A Guide for the Patient and Family* (Interactive Therapeutics, Stow, OH).

Lorman, J. (1998). *Swallowing Problems: A Guide for the Patient and Family* (Interactive Therapeutics, Stow, OH).

Lyon, J. G. (1997). *Coping with Aphasia* (Singular Publishing Group, San Diego).

Mace, N., and Rabins, P. (1981). *The 36-Hour Day: A Family Guide to Caring for Persons with Alzheimer's Disease and Related Dementing Illness* (Johns Hopkins University Press, Baltimore).

Nassif, J. (1985). *The Home HealthCare Solution: A Complete Consumer Guide* (Harper and Row, New York).

*The Road Ahead: A Stroke Recovery Guide*, 2nd ed. (1992) (National Stroke Association, Englewood, CO).

Weiner, F., Lee, M., and Bell, H. (1994). *Recovering at Home After a Stroke* (Berkley Publishing Group, New York).

# *Treatment Procedures*

# Chapter 6

# Treatment Procedures

## PRINCIPLES OF THERAPY

The majority of our patients and their families are "medically naive." They have very little knowledge or understanding of hospitals, doctors, or neurology. They may have known a relative, friend, or neighbor who had a stroke, but they really know very little about what happened to them personally. A primary role of the therapist is to explain and interpret for the patient and family; to provide them with INFORMATION.

Rosenbek, LaPointe, and Wertz (1989) clearly and profoundly state the goals of therapy with aphasic patients:

1. To assist people to regain as much communication as their brain damage allows and their needs drive them to.

2. To help them learn how to compensate for residual deficits.

3. To help them learn to live in harmony with the differences between the way they were and the way they are. (p. 131)

Paraphrased, that means that the three overriding goals of therapy are: (1) to fix what can be fixed, (2) to compensate for what can't be fixed, and (3) to teach the patient and family to cope with the differences between the way things were before the stroke and the way they will be for the rest of their lives. Appropriate goals for therapy will be for the patient and family to make the best use possible of whatever communication potential the patient has left after the CVA.

# THE REALITIES OF RECOVERY

Pierce (1995) discusses the realities of recovery in an article about her own experiences with a CVA. The therapist must fully understand these points and must explain them to the patient and the caregivers.

**Fatigue**. Following a stroke or a surgical procedure, the body uses all of the energy it can generate just to heal itself. A patient who is still physically recovering will not have the energy resources to be involved in a rigorous program of physical, occupational, and speech therapy. The therapists and family need to understand the devastating effects of fatigue. Work with the patient for short periods of time when the patient is most alert and well-rested. Also make the family aware that when half of the body is paralyzed, every "simple" task — like bathing, dressing, eating, even getting out of bed — takes twice as much time and three times as much energy.

**Emotional Lability and Profanity**. It is important to explain to the patient and family why the patient laughs and cries and curses inappropriately. Family members are bewildered and embarrassed when the patient cries frequently and with little apparent reason. They report that the patient is "so depressed," and often that friends, neighbors, and other relatives have stopped coming to visit because seeing them triggers these inappropriate tears. We do not fully understand why patients laugh, cry, and use profanity; however, these behaviors occur frequently enough for us to know that they are "normal" and "natural" concomitants of neurological injury. The two most obvious explanations are: (1) medications that actually do have a "depressant effect" on the patient, and (2) that the stroke itself, which resulted in speech–language impairment and physical incapacity, also affected the parts of the brain which INHIBIT inappropriate laughing and crying.

**Loss of Dignity**. Not only must the patient cope with inability to communicate, paralysis of body parts, and the devastating effects of sudden onset, but the whole hospitalization experience has robbed the patient of dignity. Having to rely on family members and strangers to assist with bodily functions and needs can be devastating for the patient. The role of the therapist is to encourage the patient to do as much for himself as possible and to encourage the family to allow the patient to be as self-sufficient as possible. Families most often err in the direction of being too helpful and overprotective of the patient.

**Progress Will Be Slow**. The patient and the family are so consumed with the things the patient cannot do that they lose sight of the things the patient can do. It is very helpful to use this analogy: "Your recovery from the stroke will be similar to watching your children growing taller when they were young. When you were with them all day every day, you really couldn't see them grow taller, but Aunt Susie, who only saw them every six months, always said, 'Look how much they've grown.' Recovery from your stroke will be slow but steady. You may not realize your improvement from day to day, but someone who sees you only once a week or once a month will be able to tell how much better and stronger you are getting." A key role of the therapist is to point out to the patient and family the progress the patient is making.

**Complete Recovery Does Not Happen.** In our textbooks and training programs, much material is devoted to the first and second goals: to fix what can be fixed and to compensate for what can't be fixed. Through patient and family education and counseling, we must address the third goal: to learn how to live in harmony with the differences between the way they were and the way they will be for the rest of their lives. A portion of each treatment session should be devoted to patient and family counseling.

# GUIDELINES FOR THE CLINICIAN

The speech–language pathologist serves a dual role of working with the patient to restore functional communication and working with the caregivers (e.g., spouse, family members, sitter) to help them understand the patient's abilities and disabilities and to teach them effective ways to communicate with the patient. The following guidelines will assist the therapist in maximizing effectiveness of treatment (reprinted with permission from Pierce, 1994):

1. **Work in a quiet room, free from distractions.** In home health, this most often means "turn off the TV." It is good to have the caregiver observe the treatment session — if that person can observe without interrupting or distracting the patient.

2. **Speak slowly and concretely to the patient.** Making "subtle" or ambiguous remarks may confuse and frustrate the patient.

3. **Take your cues from the patient about "space."** Generally it is best to work close to the patient but let the patient determine how close. The same is true with touch. It will vary with individuals whether or not they want to be touched. Be alert for the nonverbal cues from the patient about proximity and touch.

4. **Select treatment material carefully so that it is just at and slightly above the patient's ability.** Always start and end each session with a task that the patient can do successfully. Structure therapy so that it is consistently moving the patient forward toward as much independence and functional use of communication as possible.

5. **If a task is too difficult, shift to another task or back down to a level where the patient can be successful.** Avoid frustration as much as possible.

6. **Involve the patient in planning therapy.** Make activities relevant to the patient's interests and experiences, as well as to his/her needs.

7. **Give the patient time to respond.** Processing time for both receiving and generating messages may be reduced. The therapist must be alert to know when to repeat, and when to rephrase.

8. **Don't interrupt the flow by verbally praising good responses.** Use nonverbal reinforcement, such as smiles, touch, and head nods.

9. **Do "confrontational naming" therapy in a non-confrontational manner.** You are not "teaching" them the concept of "car" but strategies to successfully retrieve those words that they know but have difficulty recalling or retrieving.

10. **Therapy is TEACHING.** Marking +/– on a response sheet is TESTING. If you just measure 36% correct responses or 82% correct responses, you are just testing not teaching. We need to document; we need to assess progress — but don't forget to TEACH.

# THERAPY FOR AUDITORY COMPREHENSION DEFICITS

A patient who is having difficulty following directions or responding appropriately to questions may be experiencing difficulty understanding what others are saying to him. The patient with Wernicke's Aphasia does not monitor his own speech or the speech of others. This type of patient may need assistance with auditory comprehension.

According to Rosenbek *et al.* (1989), "aphasic auditory comprehension deficit is a deficiency in the ability to process or understand spoken language that cannot be accounted for by peripheral sensory deficit, generalized cognitive deficit, or primary disturbances in attention or arousal" (p. 142).

There are several components that comprise auditory skills: discrimination, association, categorization, recall, and memory. It may be difficult to identify precisely which components are impaired because of the difficulty of isolating and testing the various components. Diagnostic probing requires either a verbal or a nonverbal response. The clinician can observe, measure, and document output — whether the responses are verbal, gestural, or written — but can only make inferences about comprehension. The clinician cannot know for certain exactly what the patient is perceiving. Nevertheless, it will be important to estimate which components are impaired to plan the most appropriate treatment tasks.

Certain patterns of impairment have been described in the literature (Brookshire, 1972, 1978; LaPointe *et al.*, 1974; Rosenbek *et al.*, 1989). Patients may exhibit the auditory deficits described in Figure 7.

Often in the home health setting, little attention is directed toward remediation of auditory comprehension deficits, although most patients with aphasia will have some degree of impairment. Treatment goals are generally focused toward output responses, indirectly addressing input.

Some specific suggestions to the therapist and the family are as follows:

1. **Speak slowly.** Slow down rate of speaking by inserting pauses between the key elements in the message. This will assist the patient in "chunking," which is the processing and storing of the message in meaningful units.

2. **Alert the patient to the task.** Use a cue word such as "listen" or "ready" to arouse the patient's awareness of the stimulus.

| | | |
|---|---|---|
| 1. | **Slow Rise Time** | Represented by the individual who misses the first few units of information, then performs efficiently. The patient "tunes in" slowly when asked to respond to auditory commands and responds correctly only to the final portions of a message. Short commands may be missed entirely. |
| 2. | Noise Build-Up | More accurate performance on the first part of a message, with increasing difficulty in series of words or commands. |
| 3. | Information Processing Lag | Alternately accurate and inaccurate performance within a message. Better performance on first and last portions apparently caused by inability to receive and process at the same time. |
| 4. | Intermittent Auditory Imperception | Fading in and out in apparently random fashion. |
| 5. | Capacity Deficit | Limited number of units that can be processed. Performance seems to drop off at about the same point in longer messages. |
| 6. | Retention Deficit | Difficulty in holding material over time. Best tested by presenting material, imposing a delay, and then requiring a response. |

**Figure 7 –
Auditory Deficits.**

Reprinted with permission
from Rosenbek *et al.*, (1989).

3. **Stress keywords.** This is accomplished by increasing the volume and duration of key elements. It is not helpful to exaggerate mouth movements or to shout at the patient.

4. **Add supplementary information as needed** by gesturing or writing down the keywords.

5. **Repeat the message if the patient appears not to have understood you.** Rephrase it if necessary.

6. **Allow the patient time to process and respond.** Do not repeat, rephrase, or add supplementary information until the patient has had the opportunity to respond.

7. **Manipulate the number and complexity of stimuli presented.** Vary the field of choices according to the patient's ability.

8. **Proceed from concrete (objects) to abstract (pictures).** This progression is necessary in the target words and concepts chosen for treatment tasks.

Fawcus *et al.* (1983/1988) give excellent information on selecting materials and activities for working with auditory comprehension problems. They outline a hierarchy of tasks for different levels of impairment. The emphasis should be on functional comprehension and relies heavily on role-playing. The authors stress that "pass the salt," used in the context of a role-playing situation such as mealtime, is a more effective therapy technique than "point to salt" with objects or pictures displayed.

The *Therapy Guide for Language and Speech Disorders*, Vol. 1 (1977), by Kathryn Kilpatrick and Cynthia Jones, contains a variety of traditional activities for remediating auditory comprehension deficits. Each section provides a continuum of stimulus activities from relatively easy to more difficult. Targeted skill areas include:

1. Pointing to pictures: common objects, body parts, clothing, letters, and written words.

2. "Yes–No" questions.

3. Following directions.

4. Listening to stories and answering questions.

## Goals

The goals for therapy to improve auditory comprehension should be:

1. To teach caregivers techniques of communicating with the patient to facilitate communication.

2. To improve the patient's auditory skills.

3. To teach the patient strategies that will help to compensate for difficulties.

These strategies include the use of gestures (shrugging shoulders), facial expression (frowning), or verbally asking the speaker to repeat or to speak more slowly.

## ESSENTIAL TEXTBOOKS

Heightening auditory comprehension for aphasic patients, by R. C. Marshall, in *Language Intervention Strategies in Adult Aphasia*, edited by R. Chapey, pp. 297–328 (Williams & Wilkins, Baltimore, 1981).

*Working With Aphasic Clients: A Practical Guide to Therapy for Aphasia*, by Margaret Fawcus, Margaret Robinson, Judith Williams, and Roberta Williams (Winslow Press, Oxfordshire, England [1983], and Communication Skill Builders, Tucson [1988]).

## ESSENTIAL TREATMENT MATERIALS

*Therapy Guide for Language and Speech Disorders*, Vol. 1: *A Selection of Stimulus Materials*, by Kathryn Kilpatrick and Cynthia Jones (Visiting Nurse Service, Akron, 1977).

*Language Rehabilitation: Auditory Comprehension*, by James Martinoff, Rosemary Martinoff, and Virginia Stokke (Pro-Ed, Austin, Texas, 1981).

# THERAPY FOR READING COMPREHENSION DEFICITS

Impairment in reading ability as a result of neurological damage is called *dyslexia*. The damage may be caused by a CVA or head injury. The methods for testing and treating acquired adult dyslexia are similar to but different from methods of treating developmental dyslexia in children. The therapist should have a working knowledge of the literature for both developmental dyslexia and acquired dyslexia.

According to Rosenbek *et al.* (1989), "adults, unless illiterate, were once able to read, and had an intact as opposed to a developing language system" (p. 163). Therefore, we are dealing with an access problem rather than a learning problem. Treatment needs to be focused on facilitation strategies rather than the gradual accumulation of new skills. As with therapy for verbal expressive deficits, the therapist is not teaching the patient new information but enabling him to retrieve information that was previously learned and stored. The authors remind us that the reading impairment accompanying adult aphasia is rarely isolated and usually reflects deficits across all language modalities.

Fawcus *et al.* (1983/1988) also stress that reading comprehension is closely related to auditory comprehension, with similar linguistic and extralinguistic variables. The stimulus (written word or sentence) is presented in a more permanent way, so that the patient does not need to rely on memory to retain the message internally. However, reading depends upon visual integrity and intact connections between the eyes and the language centers of the brain. During assessment it is extremely important to identify any possible visual field deficits or perceptual problems that may be hindering reading comprehension.

Most comprehensive aphasia tests and cognitive batteries sample reading skills at the single-word level, the sentence level, and the paragraph level. If deficits are identified, further testing should be done. Webb (1990) recommends either the Reading Comprehension Battery for Aphasia (LaPointe and Horner, 1979) or the Woodcock Language Proficiency Battery (Woodcock, 1984).

Reading disorders have been classified as (1) *alexia without agraphia* or (2) *alexia with agraphia*.

**Alexia without agraphia** or *pure alexia* refers to difficulty in reading comprehension unaccompanied by difficulty in writing. Verbal language skills, receptive and expressive, are not impaired or are minimally impaired. The patient may have accompanying *acalculia* (deficit in math ability). According to Webb (1990), right homonymous hemianopsia (visual field deficit) is almost always present, but right hemiparesis is rare. The patient reads each word letter-by-letter before being able to identify the word.

**Alexia with agraphia** refers to difficulty in reading accompanied by difficulty in spelling/writing. Alexia with agraphia can be subdivided into (1) *aphasic alexia* and (2) *agraphic alexia*. In aphasic alexia, the reading/spelling/writing deficits are part of the aphasia. The reading problems tend to parallel the overall language disorder.

In agraphic alexia, which is also known as *parietotemporal alexia*, reading and spelling/writing are impaired in the absence of documented aphasia.

Before planning an effective treatment program, it is important to assess psycholinguistically the types of errors the patient makes. Some typical patterns of errors are as follows:

| | |
|---|---|
| **Semantic errors**: | close – shut<br>plane – jet<br>uncle – cousin |
| **Derivational errors**: | wise – wisdom<br>strange – stranger<br>baker – bakery |
| **Visual/shape errors**: | stock – shock<br>bear – bean<br>crowd – crown |
| **Parts of Speech**: | determine whether the errors are most commonly on nouns, adjectives, verbs or function words |

According to Webb (1990, pp. 138–139), the following principles should guide the therapeutic process:

1. "Accurate comprehension of what is read is the principal goal, not accurate oral reading."

2. "In selecting or designing the vocabulary or content, the properties or features of words that are known to have an effect on recognition and comprehension should be considered. These features are length, part of speech, frequency of occurrence, concreteness, imageability and familiarity."

3. "The patient's interests and functional needs should be of priority in selecting training material rather than what is readily available in the clinical setting."

4. "Reading should be physically facilitated by making certain the print size is large enough, the material is placed in the visual field correctly, and there are no distractions."

5. "Difficulty level for contextual reading can be advanced in two major ways: (a) increasing length and (b) increasing vocabulary as well as syntactical complexity. The clinician should consider controlling one or the other as much as possible to be able to analyze reading comprehension failures."

6. "If phonemic decoding is chosen as a useful objective, consonants rather than vowels should be targeted."

7. "Reading comprehension should be a generative process for understanding. There should be a cognitive interaction with the material. The clinician must facilitate this by the design of the treatment tasks and the selection of stimuli."

Remediating reading disorders is not often a primary goal in home health speech pathology for several reasons. The patients who have alexia without agraphia and those with agraphic alexia are not likely to have physical impairments requiring home treatment. They are more likely to be served in outpatient facilities. Those patients who would be served at home, those with aphasic alexia, generally have significant verbal comprehension and/or expression difficulties that require more immediate attention and intervention. Reading and spelling/writing remediation may be included in therapy activities designed to address problems of verbal comprehension and expression.

The home health speech–language pathologist should be familiar with materials that are available to remediate acquired dyslexia.

## ESSENTIAL TEXTBOOKS

Acquired dyslexia: treating reading problems associated with aphasia, by John C. Rosenbek, Leonard L. LaPointe, and Robert Wertz, chapter 8 in *Aphasia: A Clinical Approach* (Singular Publishing Group, San Diego, 1989).

Acquired dyslexias, by Wanda G. Webb, in *Aphasia and Related Neurogenic Language Disorders*, edited by Leonard LaPointe (Thieme Medical Publishers, New York, 1990).

## ESSENTIAL TREATMENT MATERIALS

*Language Rehabilitation: Reading*, by James T. Martinoff, Rosemary Martinoff, and Virginia Stokke (Pro-Ed, Austin, Texas, 1981).

*Therapy Guide for Language and Speech Disorders*, Vol. 1: *A Selection of Stimulus Materials*, by Kathryn Kilpatrick and Cynthia Jones (Visiting Nurse Service, Akron, 1977).

*Therapy Guide for Language and Speech Disorders*, Vol. 5: *Reading Comprehension Materials*. by Kathryn Kilpatrick (Visiting Nurse Service, Akron, 1987).

# THERAPY FOR EXPRESSIVE LANGUAGE DEFICITS

The most common and most obvious sequela of a stroke is impairment in expressive language ability. Involvement may be mild, moderate, or severe, with the severity based on the frequency of occurrence of word-retrieval problems. In the mildest form, the patient may have occasional difficulty with word retrieval. It should be noted that there is not a direct correlation between severity of aphasia and patient frustration level because those patients with "mild expressive aphasia" are often as frustrated with the inconvenience of their communication deficits as are the more severely involved.

Treatment planning will be based on the patient's responses to diagnostic testing, the therapist's philosophy and expertise, and the patient's and family's response to treatment.

Regardless of which diagnostic protocol is administered, the patient provides the examiner with a great deal of useful information regarding his/her communication abilities and disabilities. As treatment begins, the therapist will have a clear idea of the patient's

(1) type of aphasia/classification, (2) severity of deficits, and (3) strategies the patient and family use to communicate.

Rosenbek *et al.* (1989), in the chapter on "Treating Naming," discuss the major clinical issue of "whether aphasic people have a disturbance in the way their words are organized and stored or whether they have problems with accessing otherwise intact information" (p. 181).

Depending upon the clinician's orientation, treatment strategies will be based on the principles of *facilitation* or *didacticism*.

> **Facilitation**. The clinician presents stimuli in such a way that the patient can respond correctly. The clinician chooses the stimuli and manipulates the timing, order, form (whether objects, pictures, or written words), and mode of stimulus presentation (auditory, visual, or auditory-visual) so that the patient is almost guaranteed to succeed. Facilitation techniques are consistent with the interpretation that expressive aphasia results from impairment in the patient's ability to retrieve or access intact or nearly intact concepts.

> **Didacticism**. The emphasis is on teaching the patient techniques to self-cue and how to cope with errors when they occur. The clinician still selects the stimuli (with appropriate input from the patient) and still manipulates timing, order, form, and mode of presentation. Rather than chart the number of correct responses, the therapist and the patient together analyze each error for what the patient can learn about avoiding similar errors in the future or how to correct it once it appears.

Rosenbek *et al.* (1989) prefer didactic training to simple facilitation because they believe that this approach has a better chance of enabling the patient to regain stable word-finding skills. They state that facilitation techniques are perhaps best for "acutely aphasic patients who are still in physiological (spontaneous) recovery or who have not yet realized how aphasia has changed their worlds" (p. 196). Facilitation is non-threatening and can be used effectively to "jump-start" a patient on the road to recovery.

Didactic techniques teach the patient coping skills and are preferred for patients who have mild or moderate residual deficits. With this approach, the patient and the therapist work equally hard; therefore, didactic techniques are appropriate for patients who want to improve and who are willing and able to work hard for improvement. In all therapeutic settings, the clinician should be skilled at both facilitation and didacticism because different patients will respond better to different techniques.

For patients who have recently become aphasic, it is almost always necessary to begin with facilitation techniques, both in working with the patient and in counseling the family. Caregivers must be taught techniques to enhance communication.

A number of studies reported in the literature have attempted to establish hierarchies defining level of difficulty of various methods of stimulus presentation. An excellent review of these studies can be found in Rosenbek *et al.* (1989). In summarizing the results of these research studies and the author's own clinical experience, the following hierarchy of cues appears to be most appropriate for most patients:

1. **Imitation**. Watch my mouth and say the word with me (in unison) or after me (in repetition).

2. **Phonemic cueing**. Therapist provides the initial sound or first syllable of the target word. Phonemic cueing may be audible or simply posturing.

3. **Sentence completion**, referred to in recent literature as closure or cloze. Within sentence-completion activities, there is a wide variety of difficulty levels.

   a. Patients seem to respond better to a long carrier phrase ("On Sunday, some people go to ___") than to a short carrier phrase ("A bowl of ___").

   b. Patients seem to respond better when there is only one good answer ("I eat soup with a ___") than when there are several possibilities to choose from ("I eat with a ___"; "Turn on the _ .")

4. **Written word cue**.

5. **Describing by function** and/or **gesturing** the use of the object.

Different patients will respond best to different types of cueing, and the same patient may need different levels of cueing during the same session. Therefore, it is important to keep the hierarchy of cues in mind throughout the treatment session because some stimuli may require a Level 1 cue, while other stimuli may elicit the correct response with a Level 3 cue. The best therapeutic technique is to elicit the desired response with the weakest cue possible and to fade the cues as quickly as possible.

The paramount goal for intervention is to make communication as functional as possible for the patient. Speech–language therapy should involve teaching the patient to develop and use strategies that make them more effective communicators. Holland and Forbes (1993) suggest that the therapist should identify the compensatory strategies that patients have developed on their own, then help the patient to assess whether or not those strategies are helpful. Patients who have not developed strategies on their own will need assistance and guidance in doing so. Examples of strategies are as follows:

1. Signal speaker to slow down.

2. Signal speaker to wait for a response.

3. Use gestures to self-cue the response.

The role of the therapist is to help the patient use or develop strategies systematically and to be sure that family members know and utilize these strategies. Holland and Forbes (1993) stress the role of language in everyday communication. *Functional speech* includes requests, questions, disagreements, commands, and arguments. Naming pictures or objects is rarely a "real-world" activity. It is significantly easier to make speech–language therapy relevant to the patient's needs in the home setting than in the relatively "sterile" inpatient or outpatient rehabilitation settings.

*Goals*

Appropriate goals for patients with expressive language deficits are as follows:

FOR THE SEVERELY IMPAIRED

1. To establish an effective communication system by pointing to pictures or written words in a communication booklet.

2. To establish a reliable "yes–no" response system by head-shakes, verbalization, or facial expression.

3. To provide the patient and caregiver with training and counseling regarding the patient's communication deficits.

## FOR THE MODERATELY AND/OR MILDLY IMPAIRED

1. To improve word-retrieval skills.

2. To teach the patient strategies to enable him/her to become a more effective communicator.

3. To provide the patient and caregiver with training and counseling regarding the patient's communication deficits.

## ESSENTIAL TEXTBOOKS

Treating naming (chapter 9) and Treating aspects of verbal expression (chapter 10) by John C. Rosenbek, Leonard L. LaPointe, and Robert Wertz, in *Aphasia: A Clinical Approach* (Pro-Ed, Austin, Texas, 1989).

Lexical retrieval problems: Anomia, by Craig Linebaugh, in *Aphasia and Related Neurogenic Language Disorders*, edited by Leonard LaPointe (Thieme Medical Publishers, New York, 1990).

*The Assessment of Aphasia and Related Disorders*, 2nd ed., by Harold Goodglass and Edith Kaplan (Lea and Febiger, Philadelphia, 1983).

*Acquired Aphasia*, 2nd ed., edited by Martha Taylor Sarno (Academic Press, San Diego, 1991).

*Understanding Aphasia*, by Harold Goodglass (Academic Press, San Diego, 1993).

## ESSENTIAL TREATMENT MATERIALS

*Therapy Guide for Language and Speech Disorders*, Vol. 1: *A Selection of Stimulus Materials*, by Kathryn Kilpatrick and Cynthia Jones (Visiting Nurse Service, Akron, 1977).

*Therapy Guide for Language and Speech Disorders*, Vol. 2: *Advanced Stimulus Materials*, by Kathryn Kilpatrick (Visiting Nurse Service, Akron, 1979/1987).

*Speech and Language Rehabilitation*, Vol. 1, by Robert Keith (Interstate Printers and Publishers, Danville, IL, 1972/1980/1987).

*Speech and Language Rehabilitation*, Vol. 2, by Robert Keith (Interstate Printers and Publishers, Danville, IL, 1977/1984).

*Thematic Language Stimulation: A Workbook for Aphasics and Their Clinicians*, by Shirley Morganstein and Marilyn Smith (Communication Skill Builders, Tucson, 1982).

*Manual of Exercises for Expressive Reasoning (MEER)*, by Linda Zachman, Carol Jorgensen, Mark Barrett, Rosemary Huisingh, and Mary Kay Snedden (LinguiSystems, East Moline, IL, 1988).

*Advanced Communication Exercises (ACE)*, by Kathryn Tomlin (LinguiSystems, East Moline, IL, 1986).

*Daily Communicator*, by Cynthia Jones and Janis Lorman (Interactive Therapeutics, Stow, OH, 1985).

*Picture Communicator*, by Cynthia Jones and Janis Lorman (Interactive Therapeutics, Stow, OH, 1988).

*Pictures, Please*, by Marcia Abbate and Nancy LaChappelle (Communication Skill Builders, Tucson, 1979).

*Workbook for Aphasia*, Susan Brubaker (Wayne State University Press, Detroit, 1978).

*Workbook for Language Skills*, by Susan Brubaker (Wayne State University Press, Detroit, 1984).

*Workbook for Cognitive Skills*, Susan Brubaker (Wayne State University Press, Detroit, 1987).

*HELP for Word Finding*, by Andrea Lazzari and Patricia Peters (LinguiSystems, East Moline, IL, 1995).

*Just for Adults*, by Andrea Lazzari (LinguiSystems, East Moline, IL, 1990).

# THERAPY FOR MOTOR SPEECH DEFICITS

*Dysarthria*

The dysarthric patient has difficulty speaking clearly and intelligibly because of damage to the central and/or peripheral nervous systems, resulting in weakness, slowness, incoordination, or decreased muscle tone. The therapist must know the etiology and expected course of the underlying cause of the patient's dysarthria in order to establish appropriate goals for therapy. If the condition should respond to treatment, the goals will be to improve muscle tone through the use of oral muscle exercises and to improve the intelligibility of speech, usually by slowing down rate of speaking and/or projecting the voice more. If the medical condition is one that will only get worse, the goals will be to maintain functional communication for as long as possible and to prepare the patient and family for augmentative communication when verbalization is no longer possible.

Although oral muscle exercises are included in several "workbooks" for aphasic patients, there does not seem to be a rationale for incorporating muscle exercises into a therapy regimen for aphasic or apraxic patients. They do, however, serve a useful purpose in dysarthria therapy. Muscle exercises could be grouped as follows:

1. **Range-of-motion exercises**. Tongue, lip, and jaw exercises designed to stretch the oral muscles and increase range of motion while also increasing the patient's voluntary control over those muscles.

2. **Muscle-strengthening exercises**. Tongue, lip, and jaw exercises performed against resistance, such as pushing against a tongue depressor, spoon, or finger.

3. **Head and neck posture exercises**. Massage and resistance exercises to decrease drooling and assist in voice projection.

A primary task for the dysarthric patient is to learn to monitor his/her own speech production. There are a number of reports in the literature on various types of "pacing" boards and systems that may be helpful in assisting the dysarthric patient. Initially, the therapist needs to establish a cueing system that is acceptable to the patient, then teach family members how to cue the patient to "slow down" until the patient learns to self-monitor.

*Apraxia*

Similar to aphasia and dysarthria, apraxia ranges from mild to moderate to severe. Treatment techniques will vary according to the severity of the oral motor involvement. Frustration level is high, however, across the entire range of severity. These patients know very well what they want to say, but they do not know how to move their mouths to make the words come out right. Extensive patient and family counseling is necessary for apraxic patients.

The severely apraxic patient is almost nonverbal, beyond "social speech" and frequent curse words, which come out clearly. It is usually necessary to provide the patient and family with some kind of communication board or booklet initially, to enable the patient to have some control over his/her environment. Interactive Therapeutics sells excellent picture-and-word communication booklets, which patients more readily accept than poorly xeroxed pictures or word-lists made up by the therapist. Good resource pictures are also available from the Crestwood Company. The goal is to enable the patient to communicate basic needs and wants without insulting their dignity. In this author's experience, most apraxic patients are able to read at a one-word/short phrase level, so they are able to point to words to indicate needs. However, they are not able to write words initially because: (1) the right arm is nonfunctional, and (2) attempts at spelling/writing reveal the same sequencing problems evident in speech attempts.

Treatment usually involves imitation of oral motor movements, with the patient watching the therapist's mouth closely. It is far more visual than auditory. With the severely apraxic patient, it is often necessary to start at the lowest level — mā, mē, mi, mō, mōō — proceeding through all consonants with long vowels, as building blocks to reestablish functional verbalization. Less severely apraxic patients need drill on consonant blends (bl-, sl-, st-, etc.) and polysyllabic words.

The patient and family need to understand that therapy will be long-term and that they will need to practice, practice, practice. Treatment should be structured so that the therapist provides the patient and family with appropriate materials for them to follow-up on homework assignments. A series of videotapes from the Visiting Nurse Service (Akron, Ohio) is excellent for patients to practice on their own.

ESSENTIAL TEXTBOOKS

*Apraxia of Speech in Adults: The Disorder and Its Management*, by Robert Wertz, Leonard LaPointe, and John Rosenbek (Singular Publishing Group, San Diego, 1991).

*Motor Speech Disorders*, by Frederic Darley, Arnold Aronson, and Joe Brown (Saunders, Philadelphia, 1975).

*Disorders of Motor Speech*, by Donald Robin, Kathryn Yorkston, and David Beukelman (Paul H. Brookes, Baltimore, 1996).

ESSENTIAL TREATMENT MATERIALS

*Workbook for the Verbally Apraxic Adult: Reproducibles for Therapy and Home Practice*, by Karen Richards and Maureen Fallon (Communication Skill Builders, Tucson, 1987).

*Audio Workbook for the Verbally Apraxic Adult*, by Karen Richards and Maureen Fallon (Communication Skill Builders, Tucson, 1988).

*Speech Rehabilitation: A Guide to Words, Phrases, and Sentences*, by W. Chad Nye and Margery T. Tartarka (C. C. Publications, Tigard, OR, 1981/1984).

*Working with Words on Your Own* [video], by Kathryn Kilpatrick and Roberta DePompei (Visiting Nurse Service, Akron, 1986).

*Working with More Words on Your Own* [video], by Kathryn Kilpatrick and Roberta DePompei (Visiting Nurse Service, Akron, 1986).

*Working with Phrases on Your Own* [video], by Kathryn Kilpatrick and Roberta DePompei (Visiting Nurse Service, Akron, 1986).

*The Daily Communicator*, by Cynthia Jones and Janis Lorman (Interactive Therapeutics, Stow, OH, 1985).

*Talking Pictures, Kit I, II, and III*, by Sarie Leff, Ruth Leff, and James Maki (Crestwood Company, Milwaukee, 1978, 1983, 1984).

# THERAPY FOR DYSPHAGIA

Any attempts at treating dysphagia must be based upon a thorough understanding of normal swallowing and of the particular problems exhibited by the individual patient. If a Modified Barium Videofluoroscopy Study has not been done, the therapist must contact the physician and make arrangements for that X-ray procedure to be done before initiating treatment procedures. Treatment might include:

1. Muscle exercises to improve strength and function of affected muscles.

2. Positioning and posture modifications, such as sitting up straight, tucking the chin down while swallowing, turning the head/neck to one side while swallowing.

3. Prosthetic devices, such as a palatal lift or obturator or hard palate augmentation prosthesis.

4. Compensatory swallowing techniques or maneuvers that teach the patient voluntary control over closing the airway, elevating the larynx, or changing the pressure at the base of the tongue.

5. Surgical intervention, such as myotomy.

6. Thermal or tactile stimulation to trigger the esophageal swallow reflex.

7. Modification of food consistencies, adding a thickening agent to liquids, pureeing solid foods in the blender, etc.

The families of patients need to be alerted to signs of possible swallowing problems. The following pages have been designed as "hand-outs" that the speech pathologist-swallowing therapist is encouraged to copy and give to the family at the appropriate time.

# The Act of Swallowing Is Divided into Four Phases

## Oral Preparatory Phase

During the oral preparatory phase, food or liquid is placed in the mouth and the digestive process begins. With solid foods, this preparation involves chewing the food and gathering it into a bolus on the top surface of the tongue. With liquids, the oral phase involves trapping the liquid between the tongue and the palate, with the sides of the tongue forming a tight seal all around the palatal arch.

Weakness, paralysis, or incoordination of the oral and/or facial muscles may result in preparatory phase dysphagia. Specifically, the patient may not be able to maintain lip closure during chewing or bolus preparation, may not be able to move food back and forth between the teeth for grinding due to tongue, jaw, or cheek muscle involvement, or may pocket food on the paralyzed side. Others have difficulty forming a bolus or trapping the liquid, resulting in premature leakage into the pharynx (throat).

## Oral Phase

In the oral phase of the swallow, the bolus is moved through the oral cavity to the anterior faucial pillars at the back of the mouth. This movement is accomplished by elevating the tip, middle, and back of the tongue sequentially, propelling the bolus into the pharynx. Paresis or incoordination of the oral muscles can create difficulties during the oral phase of swallowing.

## Pharyngeal Phase

When the food or liquid exits the oral cavity and enters the pharyngeal cavity, the reflexive portions of the swallowing act begin. The velopharyngeal port mechanism constricts, preventing the bolus from entering the nasopharynx (nose). The pharynx and the larynx are both elevated and a peristaltic wave carries the bolus downward through the superior cricopharyngeal sphincter. The elevation of the larynx and the closing of the vocal cords prevent the food or liquid from being aspirated into the lungs ("going down the wrong way").

Pharyngeal phase dysphagia is a life-threatening condition. During the pharyngeal phase of the swallow, respiration is halted and the airway must be protected. During "normal" function, the pharyngeal phase is completed in less than one second. With pathological or neurological impairment, the transit time may be significantly increased. Portions of the bolus may remain in the pharynx and fall into the larynx when it resumes its lowered ("natural") position. Videofluoroscopy is essential to determine what is happening during the pharyngeal phase of swallowing.

## Esophageal Phase

During the esophageal phase, which is also totally reflexive, the food or liquid passes, by peristaltic wave contractions, from the superior cricopharyngeal sphincter to the stomach.

In most cases of esophageal phase dysphagia, the patient can identify precisely where the food "gets stuck." There is usually a mechanical obstruction that can be identified by X-ray and can often be surgically repaired. Neurological problems can result in disruption of peristalsis, spasms, or esophageal reflux.

# Indications and Possible Consequences of Swallowing Problems

## Indications of Swallowing Problems

A person with a swallowing problem will experience one or more of the following symptoms. If any of these symptoms are present, please notify your doctor as soon as possible.

- Coughing and/or choking, while eating/drinking or shortly thereafter

- Increased drooling or saliva

- Increased effort and time required to chew and swallow

- Difficulty swallowing some textures of food, especially meat and bread

- Difficulty swallowing pills

- A gurgling sound in the throat after eating or drinking

- Complaints of "dry mouth," not enough saliva

- Pain or pressure in the throat or chest after swallowing

- An increase in temperature within an hour after eating

## Possible Consequences of Swallowing Problems

- **Aspiration Pneumonia.** "Aspirate" means the food or liquid goes down the wrong way and enters the trachea (to the lungs) instead of the esophagus (to the stomach). "Foreign matter" in the lungs may cause pneumonia or other respiratory problems.

- **Dehydration.** If the person is afraid to swallow or has difficulty swallowing liquids, they may not drink enough to get adequate hydration.

- **Malnutrition.** If the person has difficulty eating or gets too tired too quickly while eating, they may lose weight and not be getting adequate nutrition.

# Helpful Hints If You Are Feeding the Person

1. Have the person sit up as straight as possible when eating or drinking. Chew and swallow with the chin tucked down. Tilting the head back while swallowing increases the chances of something "going down the wrong way."

2. Keep sips of liquid and bites of food small.

3. Watch the person's neck to see when he/she swallows before offering the next sip or bite. If it's hard to see the neck, place your fingers gently on the person's neck so you can feel the larynx (Adam's Apple).

4. If it takes a long time for the person to eat, serve the food in a warming dish.

5. He or she may get tired (fatigued) before she's eaten an adequate amount. It may work a lot better to serve additional "meals" or snacks during the day than trying to get adequate nutrition/hydration in the **traditional** three meals per day.

6. Avoid **baby foods** whenever possible. A list of "mechanically soft foods" is available. Most of the **regular** foods the family eats can be adapted by mashing, chopping, cutting/grinding into small bites, or pureeing in a blender or food processor.

7. If the person wears dentures, encourage them to "put your teeth in while you eat." If he or she has lost some weight recently, the dentures probably don't fit as snugly as they should. Extra amounts of dental adhesive may be helpful.

8. Wait 20 to 30 minutes after eating before lying down. This helps prevent food and liquid from traveling back up the esophagus and possibly entering the airway.

## Suggestions for Soft Foods
## Referred to as a "Mechanically Soft Diet"

applesauce

fresh fruit cut into small bites: bananas, peaches, watermelon

canned fruit cut into small bites

Ensure, refrigerated or frozen and eaten like ice cream

Nestles Sweet Success, SlimFast, Boost, or other "diet drinks"

milkshakes

Carnation Instant Breakfast

soups, canned or homemade, no chunks of meat or vegetables

chili

Brunswick stew

spaghetti

fish with no hard outer coating

macaroni and cheese

vegetables, cooked and mashed

cereal (soggy), oatmeal

eggs

puddings

yogurt, frozen yogurt

pie (filling)

---

If the person is getting fed by a G-tube and the doctor and swallowing therapist determine that it is safe to introduce **real food**, feed her small amounts of **real food** before each G-tube feeding, when she is more likely to be hungry.

Use "Thick-It"™ as needed in liquids.

## Modified Barium X-Ray Swallow Study

A special test called a Modified Barium X-Ray Swallow Study is necessary to determine exactly what is happening during the swallow. The test usually involves several swallows of three different textures: liquid, applesauce consistency, and cookie or cracker consistency. The liquid and applesauce are mixed with barium, an inert substance that shows up on X-ray. The cookie or cracker has a thin coating of barium "icing."

The MBE (Modified Barium Examination) videotapes the person swallowing each texture from a frontal and lateral (side) view. Videotaping is important because the swallowing action occurs so quickly. The team can play back the tape in slow motion, with pauses as needed, to evaluate precisely whether the food or liquid is going down the esophagus to the stomach or if even a small amount is going down the trachea to the lungs. This enables them to make the determination of whether or not it is safe for the person to swallow and to make recommendations regarding positioning and textures that may enable the person to swallow safely.

# Therapy Activities: Language

# Therapy Activities: Language

This chapter includes activities that can be used in home health treatment. They have been adapted from other therapy programs available. For more extensive treatment activities, the clinician is encouraged to purchase the "workbooks" listed under "Essential Treatment Materials" on pages 65, 68, 71, 72, and 74.

I'm hot.

I'm sick.

I'm cold.

I'm O.K.

I'm hungry.

I'm thirsty.

I'm not hungry.

I'm not thirsty.

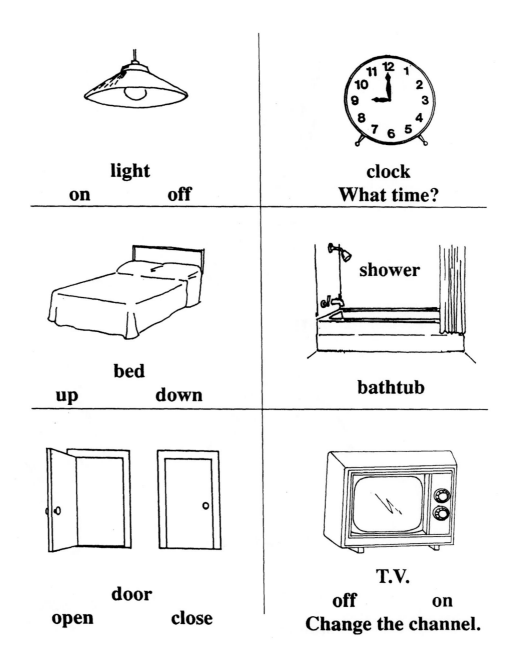

light
on          off

clock
What time?

bed
up          down

shower

bathtub

door
open          close

T.V.
off          on
Change the channel.

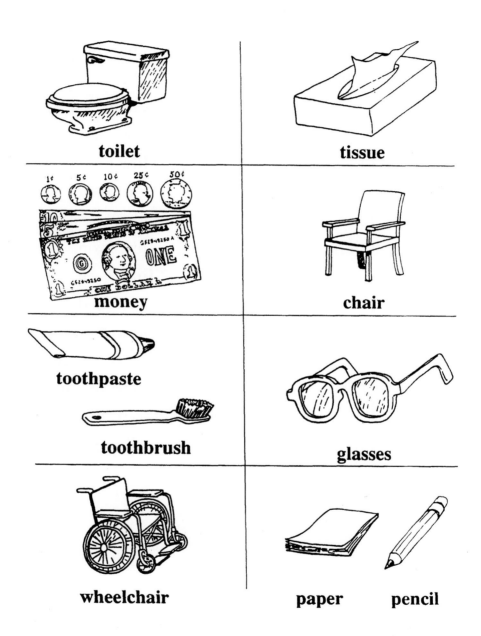

toilet

tissue

money

chair

toothpaste

toothbrush

glasses

wheelchair

paper     pencil

# FUNCTIONAL PHRASES

| | |
|---|---|
| Yes | How are you? |
| No | What time is it? |
| Hello | Where? |
| Goodbye | When? |
| Thank you. | How many? |
| I love you. | How much? |
| I'm hot. | Who is it? |
| I'm cold. | Why? |
| I'm hungry. | Turn it on. |
| I'm thirsty. | Turn it off. |
| I'm not hungry. | Go to bed. |
| I'm not thirsty. | Go to the store. |
| Come here. | Go to church. |
| HELP. | Go to the drugstore. |
| I'm sick. | Go to the bathroom. |
| I'm okay. | Call the doctor. |

# SENTENCE COMPLETION: BODY PARTS

Say or write the word which completes each sentence.

1. Wear a hat on your _____.
2. Wear shoes on your _____.
3. Wear a ring on your _____.
4. Wear gloves on your _____.
5. We see with our _____.
6. We hear with our _____.
7. Clap your _____.
8. The barber will cut your _____.
9. The dentist will fix your _____.
10. He fell and broke his _____.
11. In one ear and out the _____.
12. Talk until you are blue in the _____.
13. It's on the tip of my _____.
14. Turn the other _____.
15. Don't put your foot in your _____.

# SENTENCE COMPLETION: PLACES

Say or write the word which completes each sentence.

1.  Put your money in the _____.
2.  Buy groceries at the _____.
3.  On Sunday some people go to _____.
4.  Take the dirty clothes to the _____.
5.  Get more medicine at the _____.
6.  Have a picnic at the _____.
7.  When you're sick, you go to the _____.
8.  The airplane landed at the _____.
9.  The children go to _____.
10. Mail the package at the _____.
11. Buy a hamburger at _____.
12. To order a pizza, call _____.
13. You live in the state of _____.
14. My son graduated from _____.
15. Buy gas at the _____.

# SENTENCE COMPLETION: HOUSEHOLD OBJECTS

Say or write the word which completes each sentence.

1. You sleep in a _____.
2. You sit in a _____.
3. Put the books on the _____.
4. Remember to flush the _____.
5. The dirty dishes are in the kitchen _____.
6. Hang your coat in the _____.
7. Park the car in the _____.
8. Call him on the _____.
9. Put the milk in the _____.
10. The rug is on the _____.
11. The picture is on the _____.
12. Someone is at the front _____.
13. Take a bath in the _____.
14. Watch the news on _____.
15. Listen to the _____.

# SENTENCE COMPLETION: COMMON OBJECTS

Say or write the word which completes each sentence.

1. You tell time with a _____.
2. Read the daily _____.
3. You shave with a _____.
4. You write with a _____.
5. Drive the _____.
6. Drink a cup of _____.
7. Drink a glass of _____.
8. Please pass the salt and _____.
9. Cut paper with _____.
10. Light a fire with a _____.
11. You eat soup with a _____.
12. Wash your hands with soap and _____.
13. Sew on a button with needle and _____.
14. At night we turn on the _____.
15. Hit a nail with a _____.

# SENTENCE COMPLETION: VERBING

Say or write the word which completes each sentence.

1.  The birds are _____.
2.  The bells are _____.
3.  The sun is _____.
4.  The wind is _____.
5.  The baby is _____.
6.  The children are _____.
7.  The dog is _____.
8.  The grass is _____.
9.  The fish are _____.
10. The band is _____.
11. The choir is _____.
12. The telephone is _____.
13. The airplane is _____.
14. The snow is _____.
15. The motor is _____.

# TV SHOWS

Say or write the word which completes each title.

1. Wheel of _____
2. Let's Make a _____
3. The Price is _____
4. Name that _____
5. What's my _____
6. Days of our _____
7. As the World _____
8. All my _____
9. Lifestyles of the _____
10. Murder She _____
11. Unsolved _____
12. America's Most _____
13. America's Funniest Home __
14. Monday Night _____
15. Saturday Night _____

16. Wide World of _____
17. Good Morning _____
18. Little House on the _____
19. The Beverly _____
20. Gilligan's _____
21. I Love _____
22. Father Knows _____
23. I Dream of _____
24. The Partridge _____
25. Sesame _____
26. The Brady _____
27. WKRP in _____
28. How the West Was _____
29. In the Heat of the _____
30. Mary Tyler _____

# PHRASE COMPLETION

Say or write the word which completes each phrase.

1.  A loaf of _____.
2.  A glass of _____.
3.  A dozen _____.
4.  A piece of _____.
5.  A bag of _____.
6.  A bar of _____.
7.  A tube of _____.
8.  A gallon of _____.
9.  A quart of _____.
10. A can of _____.
11. A box of _____.
12. A cup of _____.
13. A carton of _____.
14. A pair of _____.
15. A spool of _____.

# THINGS THAT GO TOGETHER

Say or write the word which completes each phrase.

1. Salt and _____
2. Cup and _____
3. Pots and _____
4. Washer and _____
5. Mother and _____
6. Uncle and _____
7. Sister and _____
8. Husband and _____
9. Bacon, lettuce, and _____
10. Ice cream and _____
11. Peanut butter and _____
12. Bread and _____
13. Meat and _____
14. Milk and _____
15. Eat, drink, and _____

16. Eyes, nose, and _____
17. Fingers and _____
18. Boys and _____
19. Ladies and _____
20. Shoes and _____
21. Coat and _____
22. Needle and _____
23. Nickels and _____
24. Hammer and _____
25. Screwdriver and _____
26. Roy Rogers and _____
27. Dean Martin and _____
28. Romeo and _____
29. Laurel and _____
30. Dr. Jekyll and _____

# OPPOSITES

Say or write a word which is the opposite of each item.

| | |
|---|---|
| big- | rich- |
| clean- | ugly- |
| hot- | heavy- |
| fat- | hard- |
| high- | cheap- |
| fast- | wrong- |
| full- | new- |
| up- | easy- |
| left- | sick- |
| early- | straight- |
| stop- | long- |
| young- | wide- |
| wet- | quiet- |
| sweet- | thick- |
| happy- | same- |

# CITY/STATE

Name the state for each city listed.

| | |
|---|---|
| Dallas | Atlanta |
| Seattle | Roanoke |
| Baltimore | Denver |
| Las Vegas | Wichita |
| Omaha | Wilmington |
| Memphis | Philadelphia |
| Chicago | Salt Lake City |
| San Francisco | Portland |
| Orlando | Charleston |
| Tucson | New Orleans |
| Cleveland | Biloxi |
| Milwaukee | Fairbanks |
| Albuquerque | Honolulu |
| Detroit | Winston-Salem |

# EVERYDAY OBJECTS

What do you do with a _____?

| | |
|---|---|
| fork | pillow |
| comb | tissue |
| pencil | needle |
| toothbrush | belt |
| match | skillet |
| clock | hanger |
| cup | dictionary |
| telephone | typewriter |
| stove | soap |
| newspaper | wallet |
| razor | thermometer |
| broom | aspirin |
| knife | mirror |
| toaster | hammer |

# OCCUPATIONS

Tell what kind of work each person does.

| | |
|---|---|
| dentist | policeman |
| barber | veterinarian |
| mailman | florist |
| mechanic | architect |
| doctor | lawyer |
| waiter | speech therapist |
| pilot | physical therapist |
| nurse | fireman |
| butcher | garbageman |
| photographer | realtor |
| plumber | lifeguard |
| farmer | secretary |
| chef | detective |
| stewardess | accountant |
| cashier | carpenter |

## PROVERBS

Finish these familiar sayings.

1. Don't cry over _____.

2. Every cloud has a _____.

3. Don't kill the goose that _____.

4. I'll cross that bridge _____.

5. Don't put all your eggs _____.

6. A penny saved is _____.

7. A stitch in time _____.

8. A bird in the hand is worth _____.

9. Birds of a feather _____.

10. People who live in glass houses _____.

11. The grass is always greener _____.

12. Don't count your chickens _____.

13. You can't have your cake _____.

14. An ounce of prevention _____.

15. Leave not until tomorrow what _____.

# CONSEQUENCES

What would happen if _____?


You drop a glass on the floor?

You come up behind someone and say "BOO!"

You run over a nail while you're driving your car?

You touch a hot stove?

You leave the ice cream out on the counter all night long?

You wear a pair of pants that are too big for you?

Your dog gets into a fight with a skunk?

You leave the door open in the wintertime?

You pull your cat's tail?

You put the milk in the freezer instead of the refrigerator?

You poke a hole in a balloon?

You leave the flashlight on all day?

You forget to take the cake out of the oven on time?

You sit on a chair that has just been painted?

You drive too fast and a policeman sees you?

You mail a letter without a stamp?

You leave the milk out on the counter all day?

You lock your keys in your car?

You forget to water the plants?

It rains four inches in one hour?

# BRAND NAMES

What product or service does each company sell?

| | |
|---|---|
| Maxwell House: | Bic: |
| Kodak: | Oscar Mayer: |
| Purina: | Hallmark: |
| Delta: | Samsonite: |
| McDonald's: | Hershey: |
| Eveready: | Nike: |
| Lipton: | Pampers: |
| Maytag: | Nabisco: |
| Winston: | Budweiser: |
| Peter Pan: | Crayola: |
| Goodyear: | Schwinn: |
| Hertz: | Revlon: |
| Keebler: | Johnson & Johnson: |
| Glidden: | Hoover: |
| Pepto-Bismol: | Cannon: |
| Crest: | Apple: |
| Nine Lives: | Vicks: |
| Green Giant: | Tide: |
| Tylenol: | Fisher-Price: |
| Texaco: | Ivory: |

# SHOPPING SPREE

Name a local store where you would go to buy each item.

a hammer

a loaf of bread

medicine for a cold

a dozen roses

children's toys

a new car

a gallon of paint

a book about travel to Paris

a necklace

a dining room table

new tires

a refrigerator

a raincoat

a birthday card

a bottle of wine

# FAMOUS PEOPLE

Tell what kind of work each person is famous for.

Lucille Ball

Elvis Presley

Bill Clinton

Joe Namath

Liberace

Ann Landers

Abraham Lincoln

Willie Mays

Martin Luther King Jr.

Lee Harvey Oswald

Phil Donahue

Howard Cosell

William Shakespeare

Michael Jordan

Neil Armstrong

Bill Cosby

Alexander Graham Bell

Benjamin Franklin

George Wallace

Oprah Winfrey

Tammy Faye Bakker

Walter Cronkite

Mario Andretti

Al Capone

Pablo Picasso

Bob Hope

Robert E. Lee

Ringo Starr

Winston Churchill

Charles Lindbergh

Mark Twain

Ronald Reagan

Billy Graham

Clint Eastwood

Pete Rose

Minnie Pearl

Jimmy Hoffa

Wilbur & Orville Wright

Tennessee Ernie Ford

Betsy Ross

# SPORTS

Name the sport associated with each of these people.

| | |
|---|---|
| Mickey Mantle | Bobby Allison |
| Muhammed Ali | Jack Nicklaus |
| Larry Bird | Billie Jean King |
| Johnny Unitas | Bo Jackson |
| Yogi Berra | Joe Frazier |
| Olga Korbut | Shaquille O'Neal |
| Kareem Abdul-Jabbar | Peggy Fleming |
| Arnold Palmer | John Elway |
| Babe Ruth | Jimmy Connors |
| A. J. Foyt | Terry Bradshaw |
| Wayne Gretzky | Emerson Fittapaldi |
| Frank Gifford | Nancy Lopez |
| Mary Lou Retton | Rocky Marciano |
| Willie Shoemaker | Magic Johnson |
| Greg Louganis | Troy Aikman |
| Mark Spitz | Arthur Ashe |
| John McEnroe | Diego Maradona |
| Lee Trevino | Bruce Jenner |
| Scott Hamilton | Nancy Kerrigan |
| Martina Navratilova | Charles Barkley |

# CATEGORIES: LEVEL 1

Name the category for each group of items.
Add more items to each group.

1. apple, banana, orange
2. Tuesday, Wednesday, Sunday
3. nose, elbow, leg
4. kitchen, bathroom, bedroom
5. January, May, August
6. corn, green beans, potatoes
7. Nixon, Kennedy, Roosevelt
8. horse, cow, pig
9. table, chair, bed
10. dress, shirt, pants
11. red, blue, green
12. nickel, dime, quarter
13. Chicago, Atlanta, Los Angeles
14. Alabama, Texas, Florida
15. Matlock, Wheel of Fortune, All My Children

# CATEGORIES: LEVEL 2

Name the category for each group of items.
Add more items to each group.

1. collie, dalmatian, pointer
2. Popeye, Peanuts, Garfield
3. necklace, earrings, bracelet
4. tires, steering wheel, trunk
5. Huron, Superior, Michigan
6. tea, coffee, milk
7. The Beatles, The Rolling Stones, The Beach Boys
8. ferris wheel, merry-go-round, roller coaster
9. Psalms, Proverbs, Exodus
10. Hamlet, King Lear, Midsummer Night's Dream
11. Beethoven, Mozart, Bach
12. Methodist, Catholic, Presbyterian
13. quarterback, center, guard
14. airplane, sailboat, automobile
15. Notre Dame, Harvard, Stanford
16. drum, saxophone, violin
17. T-bone, ribeye, sirloin
18. Labor Day, Thanksgiving, 4th of July
19. shortstop, pitcher, catcher
20. toaster, blender, can opener

# CATEGORIES

Name as many items as you can for each category.

| | |
|---|---|
| fruits | days of the week |
| states | presidents |
| sports | automobiles |
| vegetables | holidays |
| furniture | zoo animals |
| occupations | colors |
| desserts | flowers |
| months | tools |
| farm animals | boys' names |
| body parts | girls' names |
| clothing | foreign countries |
| money | planets |

# TOURIST ATTRACTIONS

Name the city or state associated with each place.

| | |
|---|---|
| Central Park | Grand Central Station |
| Mayo Clinic | Hollywood |
| The Everglades | Lincoln Memorial |
| The Great Smoky Mountains | Epcot Center |
| The Rocky Mountains | The Pentagon |
| Yosemite National Park | Alcatraz |
| Arlington National Cemetery | Niagara Falls |
| Pearl Harbor | Smithsonian Institution |
| Statue of Liberty | Grand Ole Opry |
| Mount St. Helens | Universal Studios |
| Fort Knox | Plymouth Rock |
| The Liberty Bell | The French Quarter |
| Times Square | The Golden Gate Bridge |
| Cape Canaveral | Monticello |
| O'Hare Airport | The Alamo |
| Peachtree Street | Cape Cod |
| San Andreas Fault | Pikes Peak |
| Gateway Arch | Camp David |
| Valley Forge | Broadway |

# WHAT'S WRONG?

Find and correct the errors.

1. Please weight for me.
2. The son is shining today.
3. I can't here you.
4. Please right your name and address.
5. Hang your close in the closet.
6. You should knot go outside.
7. Who one the game?
8. I bought it at the garage sail.
9. Do you no her name?
10. He is sew strong.
11. May I have a peace of cake?
12. Those flours are pretty.
13. I have a pane in my back.
14. It turned chili last knight.
15. I bought a knew pear of shoes.

# WHAT'S WRONG?

Find and correct the errors.

1. Watch the news on the radio.
2. Hit the nail with the screwdriver.
3. The dentist will cut your hair.
4. The mouse is chasing the cat.
5. You wear socks on your hands.
6. You eat soup with a fork.
7. The quarterback made a home run.
8. The shortstop hit a touchdown.
9. The Boy Scouts hiked across the river.
10. You cook a turkey in the toaster.
11. It snows in the summer.
12. Get your medicine at the library.
13. You smell with your ears.
14. The ambulance takes people to the grocery store.
15. You cut grass with scissors.

# IDIOMATIC EXPRESSIONS

Explain what we mean when we say . . .

1. It's raining cats and dogs.
2. I'll be tied up all day.
3. It's on the tip of my tongue.
4. Don't put your foot in your mouth.
5. She got up on the wrong side of the bed.
6. She has a frog in her throat.
7. We made a cake from scratch.
8. Eat to your heart's content.
9. He is snowed under at work this week.
10. He has several irons in the fire.
11. It runs in the family.
12. That makes my mouth water.
13. He put his foot down.
14. Don't take that lying down.
15. Don't blow your top.
16. It's right under your nose.
17. It will cost in the neighborhood of twenty dollars.
18. The business may go under.
19. She pulled the wool over our eyes.
20. Don't throw in the towel.

# MULTIPLE MEANINGS

Each of these words has two or more meanings.
Tell what they mean or make up a sentence.

| | |
|---|---|
| shower | change |
| date | shoulder |
| palm | bowl |
| deal | second |
| submarine | bill |
| match | bank |
| mine | grade |
| pound | fair |
| drill | school |
| watch | band |
| jam | count |
| case | base |
| strike | prune |
| board | left |
| pool | right |
| calf | trunk |
| spring | train |
| fall | suit |
| bat | hose |
| fine | fire |
| bark | foot |
| tie | star |

# THREE-ITEM MEMORY

For lunch we had hamburgers, French fries, and Coke.
   What did we have for lunch?

In the office they have a desk, a computer, and a file cabinet.
   What do they have in the office?

I bought new shoes, a dress, and a purse.
   What did I buy?

In the garden we planted tomatoes, onions, and cucumbers?
   What did we plant in the garden?

The farmer raised ducks, chickens, and goats.
   What did the farmer raise?

We went to Spain, France, and Portugal.
   Where did we go?

We painted the living room, the dining room, and the kitchen.
   What rooms did we paint?

I bought cereal, milk, and a dozen eggs.
   What did I buy?

I went to the grocery store, the drugstore, and the cleaners.
   Where did I go?

The children went to school, to the playground, and to a movie.
   Where did the children go?

He is taking English, Biology, and History.
   What is he taking?

We recycle newspapers, glass bottles, and cans.
   What do we recycle?

# IMPORTANT DATES

| S | M | T | W | T | F | S |
|---|---|---|---|---|---|---|
|   |   |   |   | 1 | 2 | 3 |
| 4 | 5 | 6 | 7 | 8 | 9 | 10 |
| 11 | 12 | 13 | 14 | 15 | 16 | 17 |
| 18 | 19 | 20 | 21 | 22 | 23 | 24 |
| 25 | 26 | 27 | 28 | 29 | 30 | 31 |

Birthday _____

Anniversary _____

Christmas _____

Valentine's Day _____

Family birthdays:

        (name)        (date of birth)

_____

_____

_____

_____

_____

# WEATHER: FIVE-DAY FORECAST

| Monday | Tuesday | Wednesday | Thursday | Friday |
|---|---|---|---|---|
| Partly Cloudy | Bright Sunshine | Cloudy Afternoon Rain | Turning Colder | Afternoon Sunshine |
| 60 / 42 | 62 / 45 | 50 / 35 | 48 / 30 | 60 / 44 |

1. Will it get below freezing any night this week?
2. Which day will be warmest?
3. When will it rain?
4. How cold will it get Monday night?
5. What do you need to do to protect outside plants Thursday night?

# WRITING CHECKS

```
┌─────────────────────────────────────────────────┐
│                                          5648     │
│                          _____19 _____       │
│                                                   │
│  Pay To The                                       │
│  Order Of _____  $ _____    │
│                                                   │
│  _____DOLLARS      │
│                                                   │
│  For _____    _____      │
└─────────────────────────────────────────────────┘
```

```
┌─────────────────────────────────────────────────┐
│                                          5649     │
│                          _____19 _____       │
│                                                   │
│  Pay To The                                       │
│  Order Of _____  $ _____    │
│                                                   │
│  _____DOLLARS      │
│                                                   │
│  For _____    _____      │
└─────────────────────────────────────────────────┘
```

1.  Write a check to the telephone company for $36.50.
2.  Write a check to the utilities company for $81.95.

# NEWSPAPER INDEX

| DAILY NEWS INDEX | | |
|---|---|---|
| Calendar of Events | - | C2 |
| Classified Ads | - | E2 |
| Comics | - | C7 |
| Crossword Puzzle | - | C9 |
| Editorials | - | B6 |
| Horoscope | - | C5 |
| Medical News | - | B1 |
| Movies | - | F6 |
| Obituaries | - | B8 |
| Sports | - | D1 |
| Stock Market | - | D9 |
| TV Log | - | F4 |
| Weather | - | E1 |

1. Where would you find scores of last night's games?
2. Where would you find Beetle Bailey?
3. Where would you find apartments for rent?
4. Where would you find a story about a new drug for diabetes?
5. Where would you find a prediction of how cold it will be tomorrow?

# MEDICATIONS

**Coumadin**

Take one tablet
daily.

**Inderal**

40 mg
Take one pill
two times
each day.

**Aspirin**

Take two caplets
as needed for
headache or
minor pain.

**Peptid**

Take one
tablespoon as
needed for upset
stomach or
diarrhea.

1. Which medicines should you take every day?
2. Which medications do not need a doctor's prescription?
3. How many Inderals should you take every day?
4. Which two medicines work as blood thinners?
5. What should you do if a headache persists for
   more than two days?

# DOCTORS' BUILDING

| Doctors Building | Suite |
|---|---|
| Brown, G., M.D. Internal Medicine | 202 |
| Collins, C., M.D. Ophthalmology | 305 |
| Fisher, J., M.D. Otolaryngology | 203 |
| Goodman, T., M.D. Orthopedics | 201 |
| Hall, C., M.D. Pediatrics | 303 |
| Johnson, S., M.D. Family Practice | 304 |
| Lawson, T., M.D. Neurology | 204 |
| McAbee, R., M.D. Pediatrics | 303 |
| Thompson, W., M.D. Internal Medicine | 301 |
| Walker, E., M.D. Plastic Surgery | 302 |
| Laboratory / X-Ray | 101 |
| Pharmacy | 103 |
| Physical Therapy | 105 |

1. Where is Dr. Lawson's office?
2. What is Dr. Goodman's specialty?
3. Who shares an office with Dr. Hall?
4. Where would you go to have your eyes tested?
5. Where would you go for a blood test?
6. Where would you get your prescription filled?

# STREET SIGNS

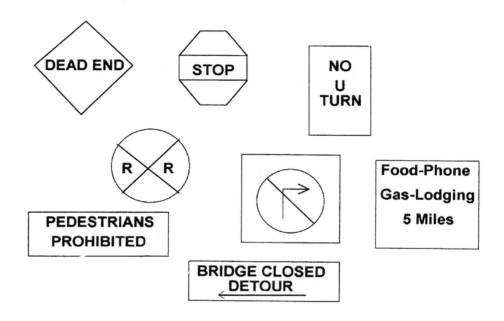

1. Which sign tells you not to turn right?
2. Which sign would you look for if you are low on gas?
3. Which sign warns you to watch for a train?
4. Which sign tells you to stop at the intersection?
5. Which sign tells you the road ends?
6. Which sign tells you to take a different route?

# COOKING DIRECTIONS

**Microwave**: Wrap corn loosely in paper towels. Microwave on HIGH for 6 minutes, rotating ½ turn halfway through cooking.

**Stovetop**: Place corn in pan of boiling water. Bring water to second boil. Reduce heat. Cover and simmer 10 minutes.

1. How many ways can you prepare frozen corn on the cob?
2. Which way takes longer?

Place one package (8 ounces) of noodles in one quart of salted (½ tsp. salt) rapidly boiling water. Cook 12 minutes stirring occasionally. Drain and serve immediately.

1. How long do you cook the noodles?
2. How much water would you need to cook half the package?

# TELEVISION PROGRAM GUIDE

## Saturday Evening

| | 5:00 | 5:30 | 6:00 | 6:30 | 7:00 | 7:30 |
|---|---|---|---|---|---|---|
| -2- | ABC News | News | Current Affair | | Feature Movie | |
| -3- | Outdoors | News | Lonesome Dove | | Dr. Quinn | |
| -4- | NFL Play-Off Game | | | | WWF Wrestling | |
| -5- | News | NBC News | Wheel of Fortune | | Feature Movie | |
| -6- | America's Most Wanted | | Highway Patrol | | M*A*S*H* | |
| -7- | College Basketball | | | NHL Hockey | | |

1.  Which channel has Wheel of Fortune?
2.  What time is the feature movie on Channel 5?
3.  Which channel is covering the football game?
4.  Which channel has national news at 5:00?
5.  What program is on channel 6 at 7:00?

# RESTAURANT MENU

## Old Chicago Pizzeria

Pizza Menu-All pizzas have cheese and two ingredients of your choice.

| Toppings available: | Italian Sausage |
| --- | --- |
| Mushroom | Pepperoni |
| Onion | Canadian Bacon |
| Green Pepper | Hamburger |
| Black Olive | Anchovy |

| Small | 9 inch | $5.45 | Extra Ingredients | $0.85 |
| --- | --- | --- | --- | --- |
| Medium | 12 inch | $8.35 | Extra Ingredients | $1.05 |
| Large | 16 inch | $11.30 | Extra Ingredients | $1.45 |

\*\*\*\*\*\*\*\*\*\*

Sandwich Menu — All sandwiches include choice of potato salad or cole slaw.

| Italian Sub | $4.50 | Pizza Sub | $5.15 |
| --- | --- | --- | --- |
| Reuben | $4.75 | Meatball | $5.25 |

\*\*\*\*\*\*\*\*\*\*

Pasta Menu — All pasta dishes are served with dinner salad and garlic bread.

| Spaghetti | $5.75 | Soft Drinks | $1.00 |
| --- | --- | --- | --- |
| Ravioli | $6.50 | Draft Beer | $1.50 |
| Lasagna | $7.25 | Salad | $1.50 |

\*\*\*\*\*\*\*\*\*\*

1. How much is a medium pizza with pepperoni and mushrooms?
2. How much is a small pizza with three ingredients?
3. Will you pay extra for a salad with spaghetti?
4. Will you pay extra for a dinner salad with a Reuben sandwich?
5. Which costs more: Coke or beer?

# Therapy Activities: Articulation

# *Therapy Activities: Articulation*

hese activities are not used as often as those in the preceding chapter, but they are included here because of their usefulness with dysarthric, apraxic, and laryngectomee patients.

# INITIAL / m /

| | |
|---|---|
| me | morning |
| milk | movie |
| move | many |
| moon | measure |
| mouth | mailbox |
| may | medicine |
| mild | magazine |
| mad | manager |
| more | muscle |
| meet | mirror |

That makes me mad.

It costs too much money.

Help me in just a minute.

Please give me my medicine.

Did the mailman come this morning?

Did they get married in March or May?

We get too many magazines.

The minister came to see me.

My mouth doesn't work right.

Leave a message on my answering machine.

# MEDIAL / m /

famous

farmer

hammer

stomach

gloomy

sermon

almost

amazing

tomato

animal

vitamins

committee

permanent

customer

remember

emergency

watermelon

thermometer

speedometer

communicate

I can't remember his name.

The committee will meet tomorrow.

My roommate is vacuuming the bedroom.

The lawnmower needs a new motor.

Lemonade tastes good on a hot summer day.

Go to the cemetery on Memorial Day.

They are meeting in Baltimore, Maryland.

Dial 9-1-1 in an emergency.

Christmas comes in December.

Grow tomatoes and cucumbers in the summer.

# FINAL / m /

| | |
|---|---|
| him | welcome |
| ham | handsome |
| jam | bedroom |
| swim | alarm |
| blame | uniform |
| come | medium |
| name | museum |
| game | Birmingham |
| arm | thunderstorm |

Please comb my hair.
I'm glad to be home.
What time will you come?
Remember to set your alarm.
The broom is in the living room.
My arm feels numb.
Jim will climb the mountain.
Tom played his drum at the game.
May I have some chewing gum?
Tell them I want ice cream.

# INITIAL / p /

| | |
|---|---|
| peace | pizza |
| push | pillow |
| pool | pickle |
| pole | perfect |
| pain | police |
| pipe | pajamas |
| point | power |
| pancake | penny |
| party | package |
| pocket | paper |

I want a piece of pie.

Please paint the porch.

Put it in my pocket.

Wash the pots and pans.

Please pass the pepper.

Don't park under a pine tree.

Take a pill for that pain.

I like potato pancakes.

He pushed me into the pool.

Pick some peaches.

# MEDIAL / p /

| | |
|---|---|
| happy | hoping |
| sleepy | super |
| zipper | diaper |
| skipper | sniper |
| shepherd | pepper |
| clapping | paper |
| surprise | computer |
| supper | department |
| open | operation |
| shopping | appreciate |

Happy Birthday to you.

She's gone shopping.

I'm supposed to be keeping track.

He was typing his report.

I appreciate your opinion.

The operator rang his apartment.

A penny is made of copper.

Poppa Bear is sleeping.

Supply the troopers with plenty of food.

The helicopter ride was bumpy.

# FINAL / p /

| | |
|---|---|
| jeep | soda pop |
| sweep | tune-up |
| deep | horoscope |
| tape | mousetrap |
| cape | cantaloupe |
| top | microscope |
| shop | countertop |
| up | teardrop |
| type | landscape |
| wipe | gumdrop |

The chicken was crisp and juicy.

Pop, throw me the rope!

Please don't slurp your soup.

Wrap the cap in green paper.

"Ouch!" I bit my lip.

Can you keep a secret?

We took a trip to the Alps in the jeep.

I need to shop for some chip dip.

Stop at the top of the hill.

Can you sleep sitting up?

# INITIAL / b /

| | |
|---|---|
| ball | baby |
| bike | balloon |
| bite | biscuit |
| bunch | bacon |
| beef | building |
| bath | bandage |
| bear | battery |
| boss | borrow |
| bones | bowling |
| bird | Bible |

A bowl of beef stew.
A bunch of bananas.
The boys bounced the ball.
Bury the bones in the basement.
I like blueberry cobbler.
There's a bee in my bonnet.
The bonfire burned all night.
I believe I'm bored.
Bathe the baby in the basin.
Put it back on the bed.

# MEDIAL / b /

| | |
|---|---|
| ribbon | somebody |
| nibble | snowball |
| neighbor | alphabet |
| table | tobacco |
| cabbage | Alabama |
| rabbit | baseball |
| hobby | garbage |
| lobby | marble |
| robber | ambitious |
| October | bumblebee |

Is anybody home?
A rabbit ate the cabbage.
Rubber baby buggy bumpers.
The cowboy roped the bull.
The robber robbed the bank.
Put the book on the table.
Strawberry shortcake.
The baby took a bubble bath.
I hit my neighbor's mailbox.
Bye Bye Birdie.

# FINAL / b /

| | |
|---|---|
| rib | disturb |
| bib | describe |
| crab | doorknob |
| tube | bathrobe |
| stab | test tube |
| robe | ice cube |
| lobe | back rub |
| cube | spider web |
| herb | bathtub |
| curb | taxicab |

Rub-a-dub-dub, scrub the tub.

Bob had a problem with the knob.

Please call a cab.

I'll have the waiter put it on my tab.

Becky ordered a club sandwich for lunch.

Put lots of butter on my corn on the cob.

Please describe what he was wearing.

Pick up the ice cube before it melts.

The bear cub is cute.

Wear a bib when you eat.

# INITIAL / f /

| | |
|---|---|
| four | football |
| five | funny |
| feel | favor |
| full | fingers |
| fudge | father |
| fire | furniture |
| phone | pharmacy |
| fall | physical |
| fat | follow |
| fast | February |

I feel fine.

Please feel my forehead.

Fall is the time for football.

Physical therapy helps me walk.

Don't forget to put out the fire.

February 14th is Valentine's Day.

My fingers feel funny.

Watch the fireworks on the Fourth of July.

Follow in your father's footsteps.

It's fun to live on a farm.

# MEDIAL / f /

| | |
|---|---|
| coffee | elephant |
| before | telephone |
| office | grandfather |
| breakfast | professor |
| awful | referee |
| careful | California |
| perfect | officer |
| muffin | scientific |
| goldfish | buffalo |
| laughing | confidential |

I want a cup of coffee.

Please answer the telephone.

Be careful and don't fall.

He's an officer in the Air Force.

Do you want a waffle or a blueberry muffin?

The speed limit is forty-five.

The professor of Finance is in his office.

Medical information is confidential.

Go to San Francisco, California.

Look before you leap.

# FINAL / f /

| | |
|---|---|
| beef | handkerchief |
| chief | photograph |
| leaf | paragraph |
| cough | layoff |
| chef | housewife |
| surf | bulletproof |
| thief | enough |
| safe | mischief |
| deaf | giraffe |
| laugh | autograph |

It is my belief that the thief used a knife.

I have enough stuff in my closet.

I'll need proof that it is an antique.

The British opposed the tariff.

They are almost finished with the roof.

Jeff pushed his car off the cliff.

My clothes are starched and stiff.

Cover your mouth when you cough.

Who's afraid of the big bad wolf?

Put your money in a safe place.

# INITIAL / v /

| | |
|---|---|
| vase | vegetable |
| van | vinegar |
| vote | vacation |
| vine | veteran |
| voice | valentine |
| virus | volcano |
| very | volunteer |
| village | vanilla |
| vacant | vitamin |
| valley | violin |

Put the violets in a vase.

Vote for vice president.

Please vacuum the floor.

Take your vitamins every morning.

Visit relatives on your vacation.

Put vinegar on green vegetables.

Happy Valentine's Day.

Your voice sounds very familiar.

The van is full of people.

I want vanilla ice cream.

# MEDIAL / v /

| | |
|---|---|
| even | reverse |
| fever | moving |
| giving | service |
| river | nervous |
| favor | deliver |
| never | everybody |
| seven | forever |
| heavy | November |
| over | government |
| cover | anniversary |

It's too heavy to carry.
Cook it in the microwave oven.
Vanilla is my favorite flavor.
Deliver this envelope to your supervisor.
You'll never dig with that shovel.
He's saving his money to travel.
The bridge goes over the river.
Was it seven or eleven?
Everybody needs help sometime.
Thanksgiving is in November.

# FINAL / v /

| | |
|---|---|
| leave | improve |
| give | retrieve |
| live | believe |
| stove | remove |
| prove | alive |
| love | survive |
| I've | positive |
| wave | attractive |
| nerve | relative |
| shave | expensive |

Please give me an olive.

Solar panels conserve electricity.

Please observe how to behave.

I can't believe I didn't receive an invitation.

I love my new stove.

Please drive fifty-five.

He needs to improve his back dive.

The mauve chair was the most expensive.

The dog will retrieve the dove.

Shove the glove into the drawer.

# INITIAL / t /

| | |
|---|---|
| tie | table |
| toe | tissue |
| ten | teacher |
| tall | toilet |
| time | tablespoon |
| tired | typewriter |
| tight | telephone |
| tongue | tournament |
| toast | together |
| talk | tomorrow |

Brush your teeth with toothpaste.
The tomato tastes good.
Take a taxi to the airport.
Toss the toys into the playpen.
Buy tacos for lunch today.
My teacher told me that.
It's tough to be on time.
Did you ever live in Texas?
Stick out your tongue.
Take time to talk.

| | |
|---|---|
| baton | butter |
| motel | city |
| hotel | letter |
| fifteen | atom |
| doctor | matter |
| dentist | heater |
| painter | sitting |
| cactus | hospital |
| tomato | better |
| totem pole | boating |

Go to the doctor's office or the hospital.

Is he a captain or a lieutenant?

I'm feeling better.

He painted the Downtown Hotel.

Please turn up the heater.

Myrtle the Turtle is my pet.

Button your sweater.

It doesn't matter.

Is he fourteen or fifteen?

A bacon, lettuce, and tomato sandwich.

# FINAL / t /

| | |
|---|---|
| eat | complete |
| night | minute |
| plate | pocket |
| foot | basket |
| taught | defeat |
| flat | forget |
| rat | regret |
| cat | ticket |
| sheet | hesitate |
| heat | appointment |

Scott bought a ticket.

I admit that he was right.

I'll bet he hurt his foot.

Please pass the salt.

She ought to pet the cat.

Don't cross the street without me.

I sat next to the man with the funny hat.

The street lights turn on at night.

Put it in your pocket.

Eat everything on your plate.

# INITIAL / d /

| | |
|---|---|
| door | dirty |
| dime | delay |
| dark | double |
| dog | doughnut |
| duck | dollar |
| desk | dinner |
| day | dizzy |
| dance | dangerous |
| dear | deposit |
| dead | direction |

Dan is in the den.

Walk the dog every day.

Dig a deep hole.

It gets dark early in December.

Deal the cards.

The dishes are dirty.

My daisies are dead.

The doughnuts disappeared.

Do you have a dime?

Don't dive off the diving board.

# MEDIAL / d /

| | |
|---|---|
| ladder | odor |
| leader | student |
| reading | murder |
| candy | muddy |
| cloudy | powder |
| credit | evidence |
| spider | president |
| headache | tornado |
| modern | medicine |
| sawdust | radio |

It's a cloudy day.
Order clam chowder.
Take medicine for your headache.
He is president of the student body.
Don't step in that puddle of water.
Disney World is in Orlando, Florida.
He is feeding the birds.
Listen to the radio.
Monday, Tuesday, Wednesday.
Put a bandage on your shoulder.

# FINAL / d /

| | |
|---|---|
| need | backyard |
| seed | blizzard |
| heard | mustard |
| bird | showered |
| stood | answered |
| hood | railroad |
| said | invade |
| hide | absurd |
| cloud | forbid |
| third | lemonade |

I need to feed my dog.

Todd walked around the neighborhood.

The child had mud on her shoes.

I can't read while I ride in the car.

Please gather wood before it gets too cold.

I watched a movie about a mermaid.

I would like to go to bed.

The crowd was too loud.

The food tasted so good.

He's in the third grade.

# INITIAL / l /

| | |
|---|---|
| look | lazy |
| light | little |
| late | lawyer |
| lock | lightning |
| lunch | lettuce |
| lots | ladder |
| last | leader |
| loud | library |
| love | lemonade |
| long | lasagna |

Good luck.

Please leave me alone.

Don't be late for lunch.

My dog likes to lick my hand.

Lock the door.

I love you.

He laughed out loud.

Please lift my leg.

Don't fall off the ladder.

Buy a loaf of bread.

| | |
|---|---|
| pilot | curly |
| olive | collar |
| pillow | spelling |
| July | policeman |
| valley | Halloween |
| Dallas | Alabama |
| silly | ambulance |
| hello | umbrella |
| jello | watermelon |
| early | elephant |

Follow the leader.

Buy a yellow balloon.

Get a gallon of vanilla ice cream.

Let's go bowling.

Yellow is my favorite color.

See you later, alligator.

He won a million dollars.

London Bridge is falling down.

She is mailing a letter.

Salute the flag.

# FINAL / l /

hall

crawl

sell

nail

file

mule

fill

peel

roll

smell

candle

recall

special

fragile

farewell

charcoal

natural

wonderful

national

crocodile

I want a bowl of cereal.

Be careful; don't fall.

I watched a whale from my sailboat.

Don't pull the cat's tail.

The girl wants a small apple.

Let's make a deal.

I'll go to the mall for awhile.

Bill yelled when Neal kicked the ball.

Peel the potatoes before you boil them.

Call me when you feel better.

| | |
|---|---|
| no | notebook |
| nurse | nervous |
| knife | nothing |
| night | number |
| nickel | needle |
| nature | narrow |
| neighbor | newspaper |
| nephew | necessary |
| Nashville | November |
| normal | negative |

Watch the news at noon.

Go Army, beat Navy!

I need a sharp knife.

Let's eat lunch now.

I'll take a nap this afternoon.

Buy a new notebook.

Please knock on the door.

What is your niece's name?

Never go out alone at night.

I need a napkin.

# MEDIAL / n /

| | |
|---|---|
| penny | tonight |
| funny | lightning |
| tennis | dinner |
| many | chimney |
| money | onion |
| picnic | tunnel |
| cannot | raining |
| finish | banana |
| peanuts | animal |
| senior | afternoon |

The University of Tennessee.

Dennis the Menace.

Put your money in the Senators Bank.

The mechanic fixed my air conditioner.

He is learning to play tennis.

The birds built a nest in my chimney.

A teenager is a minor.

It's on the dining room table.

Why are you frowning?

There is a tornado warning.

# FINAL / n /

| | |
|---|---|
| pain | again |
| mine | chicken |
| clean | cartoon |
| clown | airplane |
| chin | complain |
| spin | caution |
| spoon | begin |
| crown | fourteen |
| pine | return |
| noon | expression |

I'm fine. How are you?

Ann took the train to Berlin.

I hope the sun will shine again soon.

Hopefully, more men will join the campaign.

I've been on the phone since noon.

I'm beginning to feel the pain.

Ken got a tan while harvesting the grain.

It may rain before dawn.

The clown gave the child a balloon.

I need a clean napkin.

# INITIAL / k /

| | |
|---|---|
| can | coffee |
| key | kidnap |
| comb | cookie |
| cold | catsup |
| cook | cabbage |
| corn | college |
| coat | calendar |
| cat | capital |
| keep | committee |
| kiss | casserole |

Did you catch a cold?

Please cook corn on the cob.

My cat likes to drink Coke.

I took chemistry in college.

Sacramento is the capital of California.

Connie can comb her own hair.

You can count on me.

Carrots and cabbage are good for you.

I can't find my car keys.

Please give me a cup of coffee.

# MEDIAL / k /

| | |
|---|---|
| bacon | vacation |
| ticket | faculty |
| rocket | accompany |
| walking | significant |
| looking | motorcycle |
| circle | psychology |
| turkey | musical |
| vacuum | radical |
| chicken | economic |
| lucky | political |

Put this nickel in your pocket.

Michael is feeding his chickens.

Becky is walking her dog.

I want pancakes and bacon for breakfast.

We have turkey for Thanksgiving.

Take a vacation to Cape Cod.

I want chocolate chip cookies.

He won the Kentucky Derby.

Bill Clinton is from Little Rock, Arkansas.

I'm talking better each day.

# FINAL / k /

| | |
|---|---|
| take | stomach |
| week | mistake |
| hook | awake |
| truck | music |
| bake | headache |
| shock | attack |
| steak | lipstick |
| hike | earthquake |
| neck | terrific |
| snack | quarterback |

Luke dropped the block on the sidewalk.

I want milk and cookies for a snack.

I will look in the attic for the antique.

Check to make sure the door is locked.

Take the check to the bank.

Remember to wind the clock.

She took the notebook to school.

We should rake the yard before dark.

The truck is stuck in the mud.

Please bake a cake.

# INITIAL / g /

go

game

guess

gas

gun

goose

good

give

ghost

girl

garage

garbage

getting

guilty

garden

gumbo

gorilla

government

gallery

guarantee

Give me a gallon of gas.

Please go get my clipboard.

Park the car in the garage.

He is going to be a ghost for Halloween.

Don't kill the goose that lays the golden eggs.

Boys and girls play games after school.

Have a good day.

Get a good night's sleep.

Grow grapes in your garden.

The goat is eating grass.

# MEDIAL / g /

wagon

legal

bigger

August

tiger

gargle

forget

digging

eagle

sugar

hamburger

regular

negative

magazine

together

alligator

kindergarten

agriculture

delegation

propaganda

See you later, alligator.

The burglar left his fingerprints on the glass.

It's hot and dry in August.

Don't forget to buy more sugar.

It's illegal to keep a tiger in your backyard.

The federal deficit gets bigger and bigger.

His biography was published in the magazine.

The delegates voted to adjourn.

My grandson is in kindergarten.

I want a cheeseburger.

# FINAL / g /

| | |
|---|---|
| flag | intrigue |
| leg | fatigue |
| rag | dialogue |
| brag | hot dog |
| frog | zigzag |
| dog | nutmeg |
| bug | oil rig |
| hug | iceberg |
| dig | demagogue |
| big | catalog |

Our company has a bowling league.

I want my eggnog in a mug.

She's as snug as a bug in a rug.

The bulldog bit my leg.

I bought the rug in Pittsburgh.

My colleague gave me the new catalog.

The frog jumped from the log.

I hope the captain can see the iceberg.

Meg dropped the egg.

Give me a hug.

# INITIAL / s /

| | |
|---|---|
| seat | senior |
| sing | supper |
| sit | sandwich |
| sick | cereal |
| same | senator |
| safe | cinnamon |
| sack | September |
| socks | Saturday |
| soap | surgery |
| sign | situation |

The sun is shining today.

The sign says stop.

The sisters sing songs in Sunday School.

Please find your seats and sit down.

Was it six or seven?

Sleep late on Saturday and Sunday.

Will my soup be ready soon?

The soldiers salute the flag.

In the summer, he will sell lemonade.

The cat sits in the sun all day.

# MEDIAL / s /

whistle

lesson

person

baseball

blessing

rescue

plastic

muscles

glasses

pencil

policeman

medicine

decision

yesterday

restaurant

gasoline

hospital

grocery store

personality

electricity

Does he play baseball or basketball?

This pencil has an eraser.

He bought a bicycle yesterday.

A man's home is his castle.

The professor teaches chemistry.

We decided to go to a restaurant.

The policeman rescued the hostages.

Is it necessary to wear that costume?

Please put mustard on my sandwich.

The price of gasoline keeps rising.

# FINAL / s /

miss

kiss

choice

space

ice

race

face

mess

grass

peace

Christmas

police

express

advice

bonus

release

glamorous

generous

diagnose

dangerous

Joyce is wearing an ankle brace.

She spilled juice on her new dress.

Let's sing one verse and the chorus.

This house has a fireplace.

We need barbecue sauce, dental floss, and rice.

The price for success is often sacrifice.

Just in case, let's take the atlas.

My niece will ride the bus across town to meet us.

A mouse got in the house.

Guess what's in the box.

# INITIAL, MEDIAL, AND FINAL / z /

| | | |
|---|---|---|
| zoo | busy | is |
| zone | daisy | was |
| zebra | music | because |
| zipper | poison | noise |
| zero | present | boys |
| | visit | please |
| | easy | nose |
| | dozen | rose |
| | frozen | sneeze |
| | lazy | squeeze |

Boys like to play with noisy toys.

He goes to the cleaners on Thursday.

Please blow your nose.

Roses always make me sneeze.

Where are the scissors?

Please buy a dozen doughnuts.

His zipper is stuck.

Louise has the measles.

Surprise! You won two thousand dollars.

Spring is my favorite season.

## INITIAL / sh /

| | |
|---|---|
| shoes | shampoo |
| shut | shadow |
| shine | sugar |
| should | shamrock |
| shell | shingles |
| ship | shopping |
| sheet | Shakespeare |
| show | sheriff |
| shoot | shoulder |
| shake | Chicago |

Sit in the shade.

Please shine my shoes.

Buy shampoo and shaving cream.

She likes to go shopping.

A shark has lots of sharp teeth.

Show me your shovel.

You should wear short sleeves.

The sheriff shot a burglar.

Put sugar on my cereal.

She sells seashells by the seashore.

# MEDIAL / sh /

fishing

ocean

machine

mushroom

station

freshman

flashlight

special

washcloth

cashier

delicious

education

reservation

invitation

insurance

marshmallow

vacation

condition

population

Washington

Go fishing in Lake Michigan.

Put your clothes in the washing machine.

We got an invitation to the reception.

Make reservations for your vacation.

Shine the flashlight on the ground.

The White House is in Washington, DC.

She is washing the dishes.

They are national champions.

He is brushing his teeth.

For your information.

# FINAL / sh /

| | |
|---|---|
| push | finish |
| dish | mustache |
| fish | British |
| wash | selfish |
| fresh | punish |
| flush | radish |
| rush | toothbrush |
| brush | cherish |
| mash | foolish |
| trash | establish |

Watch out! Don't crush the rose bush.

The car crashed into the ocean.

We ate tuna fish, mashed potatoes, and squash.

The fish disappeared in a flash.

Remember to flush the toilet.

Josh needs to cash a check.

When you finish, please take out the trash.

I wish I could remember his name.

Wash your face and brush your teeth.

Eat plenty of fresh fruits and vegetables.

| | |
|---|---|
| chew | children |
| chalk | chicken |
| chair | chili |
| chain | chestnut |
| chest | checkers |
| church | cherry |
| chin | chimney |
| cheese | chuckle |
| change | China |
| choose | chocolate |

Do you like cheddar cheese?

Charlie has a big chin.

Please buy chocolate chip cookies.

Write a check to the butcher.

Let's play Chinese checkers.

Please give me some chewing gum.

Children should be quiet in church.

Don't choke on your cherry pie.

Choose a chair that is comfortable.

Please change the channel.

| | |
|---|---|
| teacher | stitches |
| preacher | stretcher |
| pitcher | scratching |
| catcher | searching |
| matches | approaching |
| crutches | researcher |
| butcher | merchandise |
| watching | achievement |
| reaching | sandwiches |
| statue | adventure |

The pitcher threw the ball to the catcher.

Did they capture the hijacker?

Mr. Mitchell is catching a cold.

Take a picture of that statue.

Do you want catsup for your French fries?

Is he on crutches or in a wheelchair?

The butcher is cutting pork chops.

Richard can't reach the matches.

The Chattanooga ChooChoo is going to Richmond.

I bought a patchwork quilt and matching curtains.

# FINAL / ch /

| | |
|---|---|
| touch | approach |
| much | light switch |
| itch | sandwich |
| speech | bewitch |
| teach | detach |
| ouch | impeach |
| snatch | dude ranch |
| rich | wrist watch |
| such | avalanche |
| patch | butterscotch |

She baked a batch of cookies from scratch.
For lunch, I want a sandwich.
Don't spill bleach on the couch!
He loves to preach in church.
The bird had its perch in the birch tree.
The paper required much research.
The coach will teach the boy to pitch.
Let's go to the beach in March.
I can't reach it.
My speech is getting much better.

# INITIAL / j /

| | |
|---|---|
| jar | jelly |
| judge | jello |
| joke | justice |
| job | joyful |
| jog | gesture |
| jaw | gentleman |
| juice | general |
| jump | Germany |
| just | jewelry |
| join | jeopardy |

Jack and Jill went up the hill . . .
It gets hot in June, July, and August.
The children jumped for joy.
Janet wants a peanut butter and jelly sandwich.
Jog around the gym.
Jim bought a jar of orange juice.
That pile of mail is just junk.
Joe flies a jumbo jet.
John got a job in Georgia.
The jaguar lives in the jungle.

# INITIAL / y /

yes

year

yard

yarn

yawn

you

your

young

yield

yeast

yellow

Yankee

yo-yo

yogurt

useful

united

uniform

yesterday

lawyer

senior

Happy New Year.

I love you.

He came to see me yesterday.

I used to live in New York.

Is he a junior or a senior?

The United States of America.

Cover your mouth when you yawn.

Is it in the back yard or the front yard?

I usually go to bed early.

Please buy some yellow yarn.

# INITIAL / w /

work

well

want

walk

warm

wake

word

worse

won – one

wipe

water

window

weekend

welcome

weather

Wednesday

wedding

woman

worry

wonderful

I want a drink of water.

The nurse comes once a week.

Please wash my hair.

I wish I could walk around the block.

Will we have warm weather this weekend?

Waste not, want not.

I'm too weak to wave good-bye.

Wake up and wash your face.

We went around the world.

I want to work on those words.

# INITIAL / r /

| | |
|---|---|
| reach | rainbow |
| rest | rabbit |
| road | railroad |
| wreck | ready |
| run | refuse |
| roof | repeat |
| wrist | respect |
| roses | remember |
| right | relatives |
| ring | restaurant |

They are running in a race.
Dinner is ready.
He's a rock and roll singer.
It's on the right side of the road.
Read the daily paper.
I don't remember her name.
Ring Around the Rosie.
Please don't rush me.
That's a good reason.
I need to rest.

# MEDIAL / r /

carrot

arrow

around

boring

earring

forest

garage

hurry

parents

sorry

battery

strawberry

cereal

insurance

paralyzed

referee

casserole

guarantee

decorated

military

I'm very sorry.

Reading, writing, and arithmetic.

Watch the Rose Bowl parade.

May I borrow your ladder?

My birthday is tomorrow.

Don't worry about it.

Park the car in the garage.

Read me a story.

How many calories does it have?

My wrist watch needs a new battery.

# FINAL / r /

wire

bar

hair

care

car

clear

fire

tear

star

scare

outdoor

ignore

beware

drugstore

explore

nightmare

before

admire

appear

sincere

We're going outside for a breath of fresh air.

I hope they can repair my tire.

The cashier broke the jar.

A fire is nice at this time of year.

Did the bear scare you?

The smoke from the cigar made my throat sore.

Where are you going tomorrow?

The bridesmaids will wear flowers in their hair.

The radar warned of severe weather later.

The rice fell onto the floor of the store.

## INITIAL / h /

| | |
|---|---|
| he | hammer |
| who | history |
| horn | hello |
| hear | headache |
| heart | healthy |
| hate | husband |
| hang | hundred |
| hope | Halloween |
| half | hospital |
| horse | hurricane |

Hi, how are you today?

My head hurts.

He is my hero.

The horse pulled a heavy load.

These words are hard to say.

Did you hear him?

Go to the hospital if you have a heart attack.

He hit the nail with a hammer.

Who ate the whole box of candy?

I hope you have a happy birthday.

think                    thank you
thing                    thoughtful
thin                     thunder
thought                  thirsty
thorn                    thirteen
thaw                     theater
thumb                    Thursday
third                    therapy
three                    thermometer
throat                   thoroughly

I'm fine, thank you.

The nurse will be back Thursday.

I thought you brought the thermos.

That makes me thirsty.

The thermometer is broken.

I think I can. I think I can.

It cost thirty thousand dollars.

Thelma sucks her thumb.

We had a thunderstorm on Thanksgiving.

That book is thick.

# MEDIAL / th /

nothing

something

anything

everything

birthday

bathroom

healthy

wealthy

author

ethics

toothbrush

toothpaste

toothpick

sympathy

arithmetic

cathedral

Methodist

Catholic

marathon

stethoscope

The bathtub is in the bathroom.

Timothy ate everything on his plate.

Nathan ate nothing on his plate.

I'd rather be healthy than wealthy.

Put toothpaste on my toothbrush.

Happy birthday to you.

The author is an authority on ethics.

Cathy is a speech pathologist.

Dorothy went from Ithaca to Athens.

There was an earthquake in California.